Adult
Attachment

SAGE SERIES ON CLOSE RELATIONSHIPS

Series Editors
Clyde Hendrick, Ph.D., and
Susan S. Hendrick, Ph.D.

In this series...

Adult Attachment

Judith Feeney
Patricia Noller

Sage
Series
on Close
Relationships

SAGE Publications
International Educational and Professional Publisher
Thousand Oaks   London   New Delhi

For information address:

SAGE Publications, Inc.
2455 Teller Road
Thousand Oaks, California 91320
E-mail: order@sagepub.com

SAGE Publications Ltd.
6 Bonhill Street
London EC2A 4PU
United Kingdom

SAGE Publications India Pvt. Ltd.
M-32 Market
Greater Kailash I
New Delhi 110 048 India

Printed in the United States of America

Library of Congress Cataloging-in-Publication Data

Feeney, Judith
  Adult attachment / Judith Feeney, Patricia Noller.
    p. cm. — (Sage series on close relationships)
  Includes bibliographical references (p.   ) and index.
  ISBN 0-8039-7223-7 (cloth: alk. paper). — ISBN 0-8039-7224-5
(pbk.: alk. paper).
    1. Attachment behavior. 2. Attachment behavior in children.
  3. Interpersonal relations. 4. Intimacy (Psychology)
  I. Noller, Patricia. II. Title. III. Series.
  BF575.A86F44   1996
  155.6—dc20   96-4527
                                                      CIP

This book is printed on acid-free paper.

99 10 9 8 7 6 5 4

Production Editor: Michèle Lingre   Typesetter: Marion S. Warren

Contents

❦

Series Editors' Introduction

When we first began our work on love attitudes more than a decade ago, we did not know what to call our research area. In some ways it represented an extension of earlier work in interpersonal attraction. Most of our scholarly models were psychologists (though sociologists had long been deeply involved in the areas of courtship and marriage), yet we sometimes felt as if our work had no professional "home." That has all changed. Our research not only has a home but also has an extended family, and the family is composed of relationship researchers. During the past decade the discipline of close relationships (also called personal relationships and intimate relationships) has emerged, developed, and flourished.

Two aspects of close relationships research should be noted. The first is its rapid growth, resulting in numerous books, journals, handbooks, book series, and professional organizations. As fast as the field grows, the demand for even more research and knowledge seems to be ever increasing. Questions about close, personal relationships still far exceed answers. The second noteworthy aspect of the new discipline of close relationships is its interdisciplinary nature. The field owes its vitality to scholars from communications, family studies and human development, psychology (clinical, counseling, developmental, social), and sociology, as well as other disciplines such as nursing and social work. It is this interdisciplinary wellspring that gives close relationships research its diversity and richness, qualities that we hope to achieve in the current series.

The Sage Series on Close Relationships is designed to acquaint diverse readers with the most up-to-date information about various topics in close relationships theory and research. Each volume in the series covers a particular topic or theme in one area of close relationships. Each book reviews the particular topic area, describes contemporary research in the area (including the authors' own work, where appropriate), and offers some suggestions for interesting research questions and/or real world applications related to the topic. The volumes are designed to be appropriate for students and professionals in communication, family studies, psychology, sociology, and social work, among others. A basic assumption of the series is that the broad panorama of close relationships can best be portrayed by the authors from multiple disciplines, so that the series cannot be "captured" by any single disciplinary bias.

Attachment Theory is one of the most popular theoretical perspectives currently influencing close relationships research. Based on the foundational work of John Bowlby and others, research on attachment has burgeoned in the last decade. In the current volume, Judith Feeney and Patricia Noller integrate some of the early infant and child attachment work with the more recent research on adult attachment, highlighting both continuities and discontinuities between them. This book presents theoretical and empirical work on attachment, issues of conceptualization and measurement, the relationship between attachment and working models, and links between attachment and other central life tasks such as work and faith.

In this extremely interesting and well-written volume, Feeney and Noller draw together the diverse strands of attachment research into a coherent account of attachment as it exists today.

CLYDE HENDRICK
SUSAN S. HENDRICK
SERIES EDITORS

Preface

This book provides an overview of theory and research into adult attachments, with particular emphasis on dating and marital relationships. An overarching theme of the work discussed in this book is that the individual's early social experiences tend to influence the quality of later intimate relationships, and that this influence can be explained, in part, in terms of the memories and expectations to which those early experiences give rise. Given the fact that the quality of intimate relationships is a key determinant of subjective well-being, these concepts are clearly of both theoretical and practical importance.

Chapter 1 lays the foundation by examining the nature of infant attachments—that is, the bonds that are formed between infants and their primary caregivers. We note the contributions made by Bowlby's (1969, 1973, 1980) seminal work on attachment and loss and by Ainsworth's (1979) observational studies of infant-mother dyads. We discuss major research issues in this area, such as the stability of infant attachment styles, and present arguments that support the concept that "pair bonds" between adults meet the criteria of attachment relationships.

In Chapter 2, we discuss Hazan and Shaver's (1987; Shaver & Hazan, 1988; Shaver, Hazan, & Bradshaw, 1988) pioneering studies of romantic love as an attachment process, which related self-reports of attachment style to memories of childhood relationships with parents and to the quality of current love relationships. We then present some of the early empirical studies of adult attachment stimulated by Hazan and Shaver's work; these studies were selected to illustrate the major research directions emerging in this area.

Chapter 3 deals with the conceptualization and measurement of adult attachment. These issues have been very prominent in this area, as researchers have struggled to define exactly what is meant by adult attachment style. We discuss the various attempts to develop reliable and valid measures and address central questions concerning the extent to which adult attachment behavior reflects stable characteristics of the individual, as opposed to current relationship functioning.

In Chapter 4, we outline two important developments that we see as strengthening the theoretical basis of adult attachment research. The first involves establishing the functions of attachment in adulthood; this work emphasizes the parallels between the functions of infant and adult attachment behavior. The second development focuses on the conditions under which attachment behavior is likely to be elicited; the emphasis on the role of stress in eliciting such behavior again provides a neat analogy with the infant work.

Chapter 5 presents theoretical work linking attachment style with working models of self and others. The concept of working models is central to attachment theory because the mental representations embodied in working models are seen as providing continuity between early attachment experiences and later relationships. In this chapter, we also explore the link between attachment style and patterns of communication, both with primary caregivers and with later relationship partners.

In Chapter 6, we outline some research questions that show the broad scope of attachment theory. These questions include how attachment, caregiving and sexuality are integrated in prototypical romantic love and how attachment style is linked with concepts such as personality and well-being. We also take up some issues concerning gender differences, without which no explanation of adult relationship behavior would be complete.

Finally, Chapter 7 deals with some applications and future research directions. Just as Bowlby's work on infant attachment has had a major influence on theory and practice, we think that adult attachment theory will make a lasting contribution to the study of such phenomena as attraction between individuals, the development of relationships, and conflict within couples. This research area is still in its infancy, however, and we also discuss a number of methodological issues that researchers need to consider more seriously.

We have found the task of integrating the rapidly growing research in adult attachment both rewarding and exciting. In preparing this volume, we have received much valued advice and support from the editors of this series—Clyde Hendrick and Susan Hendrick. We extend our thanks to them. We are also grateful to those who have been involved in adult attachment research from the beginning and who have proved themselves to be stimulating and supportive colleagues. We would also like to thank those who gave us permission to reprint copyrighted materials in this book.

JUDITH FEENEY
PATRICIA NOLLER

1

❦

Attachments in Infancy and Beyond

Recent attempts to understand adults' close relationships from an attachment perspective have been strongly influenced by Bowlby's seminal work on attachment and loss (Bowlby, 1969, 1973, 1980). Bowlby explores the processes by which bonds of affection are formed and broken; in particular, he describes how infants become emotionally attached to their primary caregivers and emotionally distressed when separated from them. Bowlby is convinced that children need a close and continuous relationship with a primary caregiver to thrive emotionally. He sees existing psychological theories as inadequate for explaining the intense attachment of infants and young children to the caregiver and their dramatic responses to separation (Bretherton, 1992).

1

Bowlby (1969, 1973, 1980) draws on concepts from many sources, including ethology, psychoanalysis, and control systems theory. His theory is also based on a broad range of observations: of disturbed and maladjusted children in clinical and institutional settings, of infants and young children who were separated from their primary caregivers for varying periods of time, and of nonhuman primate mothers and their offspring. The theoretical formulation provides a detailed account of the development, function, and maintenance of attachment behavior.

The principles of attachment that Bowlby (1969, 1973, 1980) describes have made a vast theoretical contribution to the understanding of child development, but also have had a profound influence on psychological practice. Based on the work of Bowlby and his colleagues and students, revolutionary changes were made in the care of institutionalized children. Practices in hospitals have also changed dramatically to minimize separations between parents and children. For example, mothers are encouraged to spend a lot of time with their hospitalized children and to perform basic caring tasks for them (e.g., feeding). The events surrounding childbirth have also changed significantly, with fathers now present at births and both fathers and siblings being able to interact with the mother and the new infant while they are still in the hospital. In addition, Bowlby's work has clear implications for those dealing with loss, grief, and mourning, and, more generally, for parenting behavior and child care practice. Because research into adult attachment has its basis in Bowlby's work, this chapter is devoted to outlining the main principles of his formulation and to assessing the relevant empirical evidence.

❧ The Nature and Function of Attachment Behavior

Bowlby (1973) defines attachment behavior as "any form of behavior that results in a person attaining or retaining proximity to some other differentiated and preferred individual, usually conceived as stronger and/or wiser" (p. 292). Infant behaviors such as sucking, clinging, following, smiling, and crying tend to elicit protective responses from adult caregivers and bind the infant and caregiver to each other.

Given strong parallels between human attachment behavior and similar attachment behavior shown by nonhuman primate species, Bowlby (1973) hypothesizes that attachment behavior is adaptive, having evolved through a process of natural selection. That is, attachment behavior offers infants a survival advantage, protecting them from danger by keeping them close to the primary caregiver (usually the mother).

Bowlby (1973) further hypothesizes that attachment behavior forms an organized behavioral system. That is, a varied set of behaviors (e.g., smiling, crying, visual following) serves a single function (maintaining proximity to the caregiver). Bowlby sees the attachment system as one of several interlocking behavioral systems, including exploration, caregiving, and sexual mating, designed to ensure survival and procreation. From the viewpoint of the outsider, the goal of the attachment system is to regulate behaviors designed to establish or maintain contact with an attachment figure; from the viewpoint of the attached person, the goal of the system is "felt security."

Bowlby (1973) describes behavioral systems as homeostatic control systems that maintain a relatively steady state between the individual and his or her environment. The attachment system maintains a balance between exploratory behavior and proximity-seeking behavior, taking into account the accessibility of the attachment figure and the dangers present in the physical and social environment. Infants perceive separation (actual or threatened) from their attachment figure as a threat to their well-being and try to remain within the protective range of this figure. The protective range is reduced in strange or threatening situations; hence, attachment behavior is more likely to be evident when the infant is in a situation of apparent threat.

Although Bowlby (1973) defines attachment behavior in terms of the goal of proximity maintenance, other interrelated functions of attachment have been identified. In general, the attachment figure serves as a secure base from which the infant feels safe to explore and master the environment. That is, in situations of no apparent threat, the infant is likely to engage in exploratory activity rather than in attachment behavior. On the other hand, proximity to the caregiver is most likely to be sought when the infant perceives a threat in the immediate environment. Thus, the caregiver also serves as a safe haven to which the infant can turn for reassurance and comfort on such occasions. According to Bowlby, proximity seeking (including protest at separation), secure base, and safe haven are the three defining features, and the three functions, of an attachment relationship.

The basic features of the attachment system are illustrated in Figure 1.1. The model depicted in Figure 1.1 shows how attachment and exploratory behaviors are influenced by the child's perceptions of the availability and responsiveness of the caregiver. When children feel secure and confident in the caregiver, they are likely to be more sociable and less inhibited and to engage in more play and exploration. On the other hand, when children feel insecure and lack confidence in the caregiver, they are likely to respond either with fear and anxiety or with defensiveness. Responding with fear and anxiety leads to such behaviors as crying and clinging, whereas responding with defensiveness leads to avoidance of close contact with the attachment figure.

❧ Individual Differences in Attachment

Bowlby (1973) regards the attachment system as having evolved through natural selection and considers the processes comprising this system to be universal in human nature. Complementing this normative view of attachment behavior, he also addresses the issue of individual differences, as can be seen in the following key propositions of attachment theory (p. 235):

1. When an individual is confident that an attachment figure is available whenever he or she desires it, that person is much less prone to either intense or chronic fear than an individual who, for any reason, has no such confidence.

2. Confidence in the availability of attachment figures, or lack of such confidence, is built up slowly during the years of immaturity (infancy, childhood, and adolescence); whatever expectations are

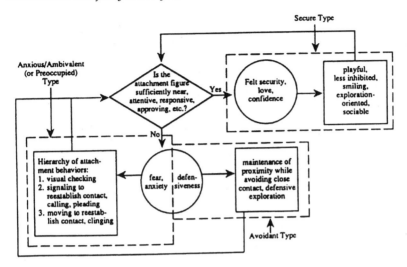

Figure 1.1. Basic Features of the Attachment System
SOURCE: Hazan and Shaver (1994).

developed during those years tend to persist relatively unchanged throughout the rest of life.

3. The varied expectations of the accessibility and responsiveness of attachment figures that individuals develop during the years of immaturity are tolerably accurate reflections of the experiences those individuals have actually had.

Central to these key propositions is the role of the individual's expectations of attachment figures. Expectations about the availability and responsiveness of attachment figures are thought to be incorporated into inner working models of attachment. Working models of attachment reflect memories and beliefs that develop from the individual's early experiences of caregiving; they are carried forward into new relationships, where they play an active role in guiding perceptions and behavior.

Expectations concerning the availability and responsiveness of the caregiver are based on two variables: whether the attachment figure is judged to be the sort of person who generally responds to calls for support and protection, and whether the self is judged to be the sort of person toward whom others are likely to respond in a helpful way. These two variables (models of other and models of self) are logically independent; because both originate from actual interpersonal transactions, however, they tend to be complementary and mutually confirming (Bowlby, 1973).

Working models of the self and of social interaction partners usually develop in the context of relatively stable family settings and tend to persist throughout life. Because working models exert a continuing influence on behavior, attachment patterns are thought to show considerable stability over time. The concept of working models is taken up in greater detail in Chapter 5. The issue of the stability of attachment patterns is controversial, however, and is taken up at several later points in this book.

Describing Individual Differences in Attachment

The first detailed studies of individual differences in attachment were conducted by Ainsworth (who is heavily influenced by the ideas of Bowlby and who, in turn, has made major contributions to Bowlby's thinking). Ainsworth conducted naturalistic observations of mother-infant interactions in Uganda and in Baltimore, Maryland; each of these projects involved intensive longitudinal data collection obtained during a series of home visits.

On the basis of these observations, Ainsworth and her colleagues (Ainsworth, Blehar, Waters, & Wall, 1978) suggest that organized patterns of infant behavior can be used to identify styles of infant-mother attachment. Ainsworth et al. delineate three such styles: insecurely attached-avoidant (Group A), securely attached (Group B), and insecurely attached-resistant or anxious-ambivalent (Group C). The patterns of infant behavior that define these three styles are systematically related to the amount of interaction between mother and infant and to the mother's sensitivity and responsiveness to the infant's needs and signals. These patterns are related to the variations in behavior shown in Figure 1.1: Group A children respond with defensiveness and avoidance of close contact; Group B children are sociable and engage in high levels of exploration; Group C children respond with anxious

Table 1.1 Characteristics of the Three Major Infant Attachment Styles

Attachment Style	Infant Behavior	Quality of Caregiving
Avoidant (Group A)	Detachment behaviors; avoidance of caregiver	Rejecting; rigid; hostile; averse to contact
Secure (Group B)	Active exploration; upset by separation; positive response to caregiver	Available; responsive; warm
Anxious-ambivalent (Group C)	Protest behaviors; distress at separation; anger-ambivalence to caregiver	Insensitive; intrusive; inconsistent

behaviors such as crying and clinging. Table 1.1 shows the be-havioral characteristics of the three styles, together with the as-sociated patterns of caregiving.

Ainsworth et al. (1978) developed a laboratory procedure for assessing attachment style based on an infant's reactions to a series of separations from and reunions with the mother and a friendly stranger. The Strange Situation technique was designed to create mild but gradually increasing stress for the infant (see Table 1.2) so that consequent changes in the behavior of the infant toward the attachment figure could be observed. The Strange Situation technique has been widely used to assess infant attachment style and to study the relationship between early attachment behavior and later social and emotional development. (Criticisms have been leveled, however, at the tendency of researchers to rely on this technique as an assessment tool at the expense of considering behavior in more naturally occurring social situations.)

It is important to remember that the Strange Situation technique focuses on the infant's behavior toward the primary caregiver when distressed by the departure of the caregiver and the ap-proach of a stranger. According to attachment theory, attachment styles reflect rules that guide responses to emotionally distressing situations; that is, attachment theory can be described as a *theory of affect regulation* (Kobak & Sceery, 1988; Sroufe & Waters, 1977). Secure attachment is thought to reflect rules that allow the in-

Table 1.2 Series of Incidents Used in Strange Situation

1. Mother and infant together in a strange room with toys

2. Mother and infant joined by female stranger

3. Mother leaves the infant with the stranger

4. Mother returns and stranger leaves

5. Mother leaves infant alone

6. Stranger returns

7. Mother returns

SOURCE: Ainsworth et al. (1978).

dividual to acknowledge distress and to turn to others for comfort and support; avoidant attachment reflects rules that restrict the willingness to acknowledge distress and to seek support; anxious-ambivalent attachment is marked by hypersensitivity toward negative affect and by heightened expressions of distress.

It should be noted that revisions to the tripartite classification have been proposed. Because considerable differences in attachment behavior have been observed within attachment groups, more fine-grained categories have been devised. In particular, researchers have identified four subgroups within the secure classification based on differences in the quality of separation distress (see Belsky & Rovine, 1987).

In addition, researchers have often been unable to classify all infants into the three attachment categories outlined by Ainsworth and her colleagues (1978). For this reason, researchers have proposed a fourth group (the disorganized-disoriented category of insecure attachment; Main & Solomon, 1986). This group tends to show contradictory reunion behavior (e.g., approaching the attachment figure with head turned away), confusion or apprehension in response to the approaching attachment figure, and changeable or depressed affect. These characteristics overlap with those defining another recently proposed fourth group: the A-C group, which involves a combination of avoidant (Group A) and resistant (Group C) reunion behavior. The latter group has been reported by a number of infant researchers (Crittenden, 1985; Radke-Yarrow, Cummings, Kuczynski, & Chapman, 1985). Both of these extra categories are particularly relevant to the classification of infants in social risk groups (e.g., maternal depression and maltreatment; see Bretherton, 1987; Carlson, Cicchetti, Barnett, & Braunwald, 1989; Spieker, 1986).

Describing Multiple Attachments

Bowlby (1984) places strong emphasis on the bond between mother and infant and tends to see the role of fathers as secondary. (This emphasis reflects views prevailing at the time; see Bretherton, 1992. Later researchers and students in the attachment tradition have addressed the bond between infants and fathers in some detail.) According to Bowlby, the child is biased toward attaching himself or herself especially to one figure, mainly the mother.

Despite the significance attributed to the infant-mother bond, Bowlby (1984) clearly recognizes that a human infant can, and usually does, become attached to more than one figure (Ainsworth, 1979). In fact, Bowlby maintains that by 9 or 10 months of age, most children have multiple attachment figures. He maintains, however, that the principal caregiver becomes the primary attachment figure and the one who is preferred as a safe haven in times of distress. Other figures are secondary and supplementary to that primary figure, with fathers and older siblings being the most common secondary figures. This formulation implies a hierarchy of attachment figures.

Consistent with this formulation, data suggest that childhood representations of attachment are related to infant attachment classification with the mother but not with the father (Main, Kaplan, & Cassidy, 1985). Thus, the principal attachment figure may be especially influential in the construction of working models (Bretherton, 1985). The comparison of attachment classifications to mothers and fathers is also relevant to the explanation of individual differences in attachment, as we shall show in the next section.

Explaining Individual Differences in Attachment

The attachment patterns documented by Ainsworth (1979; Ainsworth et al., 1978) and by subsequent researchers raise questions concerning the origins of individual differences in attachment. It has been suggested that the specific manifestations of the attachment system are influenced by a range of factors, including individual experience, genetic constitution, and cultural influences (Ainsworth, 1989).

Of these three factors, attachment researchers have focused most strongly on the first two. That is, research into the determinants of attachment quality has emphasized the roles of maternal caregiving (as an index of individual experience) and infant temperament (as an index of genetic constitution; note, however, that infant temperament may reflect environmental, as well as genetic, influences). Given the ongoing debate about the relative importance of maternal caregiving and infant temperament as determinants of attachment patterns, we will discuss these two factors separately and then integrate the findings.

Individual experience. Traditional attachment theory acknowledges that the quality of infant-mother attachment depends on the initial biases that each partner brings to the relationship and on the direct influence that each exerts on the other (Bowlby, 1984, p. 340). The theory asserts, however, that the role of infant behavior in determining interaction patterns is overshadowed by the behavior of the caregiver (Goldsmith & Alansky, 1987). This assertion is reflected in Bowlby's (1984) emphasis on the role of early caregiving experiences (see Proposition 3 in the section on individual differences in attachment) and in Ainsworth's (1979) descriptions of infant attachment styles.

A large body of empirical evidence supports the relationship between attachment quality and maternal variables. Specifically, attachment style has been related to various indexes of quality of care, such as responsiveness to crying, timing of feeding, sensitivity, psychological accessibility, cooperation, and acceptance (Ainsworth, 1979, 1982; Bates, Maslin, & Frankel, 1985; Isabella, 1993; Pederson et al., 1990; Roggman, Langlois, & Hubbs-Tait, 1987).

Recent research within this tradition has expanded to study infants' interactions with both mothers and fathers. Cox, Owen, Henderson, and Margand (1992) found that a measure of infant-mother security at 12 months of age is related to observers' ratings of the quality of mother-infant interaction at 3 months of age and to interview measures of the time that mothers spent with the infant at 3 months of age. Similarly, infant-father security is related to earlier ratings of father-infant interaction and the time fathers spent with the infant; interestingly, infant-father security is also related to fathers' attitudes to the infant and to the paternal role. These results clearly support the link between caregiver behavior and attachment security.

Not all studies attempting to relate attachment patterns to aspects of caregiving behavior have found clear relationships, however (e.g., Miyake, Chen, & Campos, 1985). Recently, researchers have argued that rigorous testing of the effect of maternal behavior on attachment quality requires careful definition of the independent variable: Measures of maternal behavior should emphasize the role of maternal sensitivity, as dictated by attachment principles (Isabella, Belsky, & von Eye, 1989). In line with this position, Isabella et al. (1989) developed a measure of *interactional synchrony*, or the extent of reciprocal and mutually rewarding exchanges of behavior between infant and mother. Their results support the association between interactional synchrony and attachment type and suggest that this association cannot be explained in terms of infant temperament or behavior (Isabella & Belsky, 1991; Isabella et al., 1989).

The role of caregiver behavior in influencing attachment quality has also been addressed by studies comparing the quality of the infant's relationships with each parent. In terms of attachment classifications derived from the Strange Situation, for example, an infant may be securely attached to one parent and insecurely attached to the other (e.g., Main & Weston, 1981). This lack of concordance of attachment relationships with mother and father has been cited as supporting the dominant role of caregiver behavior (and the limited role of infant temperament).

Genetic contribution. In contrast to the position taken by traditional attachment theorists, several investigators have proposed

that individual differences in attachment quality stem from differences in infant characteristics (in addition to, or instead of,
differences in caregiver behavior). The effect of infant temperament on attachment has been investigated using various opera-
tional definitions of temperament: emotionality, fussiness or
"difficulty," irritability, activity level, proneness to distress, and
sociability.

The resulting empirical evidence is mixed; some researchers
have found evidence for the effects of infant temperament
(Calkins & Fox, 1992; Miyake et al., 1985), whereas others have not
(Egeland & Farber, 1984). Much of the research addressing this
issue has been criticized on methodological grounds, however.

First, many studies of the role of infant temperament have
adopted a simplistic approach, relying on correlations between
temperament ratings and attachment classifications. This approach ignores the fact that infant temperament may influence the
attachment system in different ways: It may exert a direct effect on
infant-mother interaction; alternatively, it may affect attachment
behavior indirectly through its effects on the infant's separation
distress (Thompson, Connell, & Bridges, 1988). Indeed, Vaughn,
Lefever, Seifer, and Barglow (1989) found that infant temperament
is related to infant distress during separation episodes of the
Strange Situation.

Second, the role of infant temperament in predicting attachment
may depend on the measure of attachment style used. Belsky and
Rovine (1987) note that attachment subgroups can be split in more
than one meaningful way and that different classification methods
may reflect different influences on attachment. Whereas the traditional A-B-C classification shows quite limited associations with
infant temperament, observational data support the utility of contrasting two groups: one containing avoidant infants and secure
infants from subgroups B1 and B2 and the other containing resistant infants and secure infants from subgroups B3 and B4. This
grouping appears to reflect temperament factors that cut across
the secure-insecure distinction.

Vaughn and colleagues (Vaughn et al., 1992) also suggest that
different measures of attachment style vary in their overlap with
measures of infant temperament. Specifically, they note limited

associations between infant temperament and Strange Situation assessments of attachment; by contrast, assessments that focus on the salience and effectiveness of attachment behavior in daily functioning (e.g., Q sorts) show a wider range of correlates, including child temperament.

In the previous section, we referred to studies comparing the quality of the infant's relationships with each parent. A meta-analysis of these studies (Fox, Kimmerly, & Schafer, 1991) suggests that security of attachment to one parent is reliably related to security of attachment to the other (although approximately 30% of infants are classified as securely attached to one parent and insecurely attached to the other). Fox et al. (1991) note that the reason for the high percentage of concordant attachment relationships is unclear: This finding may reflect the role of infant temperament in determining attachment quality; alternatively, it may reflect consistent parenting styles within families or the overriding influence of the child's working model of attachment (usually developed as a result of the relationship with the mother).

Individual experience versus genetic contribution. To sum up, integrative studies provide evidence that both maternal variables and infant temperament contribute to attachment security (Izard, Haynes, Chisholm, & Baak, 1991). There is also evidence that maternal behavior and infant temperament may jointly influence attachment security. For example, Crockenberg (1981) shows that neonatal irritability predicts insecure attachment at 12 months of age, but only for infants whose mothers were relatively unresponsive to their infant's crying at 3 months and who received little social support. Similarly, Mangelsdorf and colleagues (Mangelsdorf, Gunnar, Kestenbaum, Lang, & Andreas, 1990) found that attachment security at 13 months of age is predicted by the interaction between maternal personality and infant proneness to distress. These findings support Bowlby's (1969, 1973, 1980) view that attachment patterns reflect the interaction between the child's personality, the family, and the wider social environment.

Conclusions about the relative contributions of maternal variables and infant temperament remain speculative. There is some consensus that the role of infant temperament is limited and that maternal behaviors are at least equally important (Goldsmith & Alansky, 1987).

Cultural influences. Some research attention has also been devoted to the study of cross-cultural attachment patterns. In a meta-analysis of studies based on the Strange Situation, Van IJzendoorn and Kroonenberg (1988) note that the distribution of attachment classifications in eight countries shows considerable differences both within and across cultures. Although the secure category appears to be modal in all countries, the relative frequencies of the two major forms of insecure attachment differ quite markedly between countries (with greater relative frequencies of A classifications in Western European countries and C classifications in Israel and Japan). It is thought that these different patterns reflect culturally based child-rearing practices.

Sagi, Van IJzendoorn, and Koren-Karie (1991) suggest that cultural differences in attachment classifications may reflect cultural differences in preseparation behavior. In other words, the initial episodes of the Strange Situation, which are designed to produce novelty and mild stress, may actually produce different effects in different cultures: Infants from cultures that encourage early independence may exhibit less stress in response to these episodes. If so, the cross-cultural utility of the Strange Situation technique could be called into question. Sagi et al. (1991), however, found that preseparation responses show few cross-cultural differences beyond those attributable to the Israeli kibbutz sample (which represents a unique child-rearing context and is marked by anxiety during preseparation episodes).

To date, most cross-cultural studies of the Strange Situation have focused on describing cultural differences in attachment classifications and attributing these differences to cultural practices (e.g., the high incidence of A classifications in Germany has been attributed to the parental push for early independence rather than to rejection; Grossmann, Grossmann, Spangler, Suess, & Unzner, 1985). Systematic investigation of parental beliefs and social practices has rarely been carried out, however (Bretherton, 1992). In addition, further research needs to assess the implications of attachment classifications for future adaptation to the demands of specific cultures (Sagi et al., 1991).

❧ Stability of Attachment Patterns

As noted earlier, attachment theorists propose that attachment patterns are relatively stable. According to Bowlby (1980), continuity of attachment style is due primarily to the persistence of mental models of the self and others, central components of personality. Working models tend to be stable because they develop and operate in the context of a fairly stable family setting. In addition, as the ways of thinking incorporated in the models become habitual and automatic over time, the models come to operate largely outside of conscious awareness, rendering them more resistant to change.

It has also been suggested that working models of attachment are likely to be self-fulfilling because actions based on these models tend to produce consequences that reinforce them. For example, approaching new social contacts with a defensive attitude increases the likelihood of rejection, which in turn reinforces insecurity (Douglas & Atwell, 1988). Sroufe (1988; Sroufe & Fleeson, 1986) further suggests that, in forming new relationships, children actually seek to recreate the roles and interaction patterns that they learned in the context of early relationships, even if those relationships were exploitive or destructive.

On the other hand, attachment theorists recognize that attachment behavior and working models cannot be regarded as fixed in infancy and unchanging throughout life. Bowlby (1980) raises several points relevant to the issue of change in attachment patterns. First, he suggests that attachment patterns vary in stability depending on the degree of satisfaction that each person derives from the pattern. Second, he acknowledges that attachment patterns (even those that show early signs of stability) may be changed by subsequent events that alter the behavior of either of the individuals in the relationship. Finally, he notes that working models themselves are subject to change; when the lack of fit between actual social interchanges and corresponding working models becomes so great that the models are no longer effective, the individual will begin the process of accommodating the models to reality.

The extent of continuity of attachment behavior remains controversial. Empirical evidence suggests that infant attachment classifications based on Ainsworth's (1979) system are reasonably stable over time. Specifically, most infants assessed at 12 months of age and reviewed at 18 months obtain the same classification at both assessments (e.g., Goossens, Van IJzendoorn, Tavecchio, & Kroonenberg, 1986; Waters, 1978).

Moreover, a growing number of longitudinal studies provide evidence of continuity of attachment style from infancy through to the early school years. Main et al. (1985) report that attachment security at 12 months, as assessed in the Strange Situation, predicts a number of aspects of attachment organization at 6 years of age, including reunion behavior, discourse fluency within the child-parent dyad, and emotional responses to pictured separations. Further, Sroufe (1988) notes that early attachment classification is related to independent Q-sort descriptions of anxiety-security and peer competence based on school observations of children in third grade.

At the same time, these studies are complemented by investigations into the correlates of change in attachment style and working models. Longitudinal studies of socioeconomically disadvantaged families suggest that change in attachment style from infancy to childhood is related to family circumstances; specifically, the families of children who change from secure to insecure attachment are characterized by more severe life stresses, and change from insecure to secure attachment is frequently associated with the availability of an additional caregiver (Egeland & Sroufe, 1981; Vaughn, Egeland, Sroufe, & Waters, 1979). Similarly, Lamb, Thompson, Gardner, Charnov, and Estes (1985) report that temporal stability of attachment is high only when there is stability of family and care-taking circumstances; this conclusion is consistent with Bowlby's (1980) views on continuity and change in attachment behavior.

It has been suggested that working models are most likely to be revised within the context of other relationships; that is, the formation of new relationships offers the opportunity to modify internal working models based on previous negative experiences (Buhrmester & Furman, 1986; Ricks, 1985; Sroufe & Fleeson, 1986).

The revision of mental models may also be facilitated by aspects of development within the individual. With the advent of formal operations, for example, the individual is able to think about attachment-related issues in a way that is not limited by his or her concrete experiences. This claim is supported by material from interviews in which adults discussed their relationships with their parents in childhood and later life and the influence of these experiences on their adult personalities (Main et al., 1985).

Further research is required into the continuity of attachment behavior across the life span and the factors that promote change. It is important to keep in mind, however, that attachment theory is not predicated on the assumption that attachment patterns are extremely stable; rather, the theory proposes a relationship between caregiving interaction and attachment quality, implying that the latter should be sensitive to circumstances that influence the extent or type of interaction (Lamb et al., 1985).

❧ Predictive Validity of Attachment Classifications

Attachment researchers have investigated the association between early attachment classification (usually based on the Strange Situation) and various indexes of functioning. Although a detailed presentation of this work is beyond the scope of the present book, it is useful to summarize findings concerning the predictive validity of early attachment patterns.

Significant relationships have been observed between early classifications of attachment style (usually taken at 12 to 18 months of age) and a number of dependent measures taken either concurrently or at later stages of infancy or toddlerhood. For example, secure attachment has been linked with exploratory play (Hazen & Durrett, 1982); longer attention span and more positive affect during free play (Main, 1983); autonomous problem solving (Matas, Arend, & Sroufe, 1978); sociability with unfamiliar adults (Main & Weston, 1981; Thompson & Lamb, 1983); open and effective communication between children and parents (Main, Tomasini, & Tolan, 1979; Matas et al., 1978); low levels of distraction and low need for discipline (Bus & Van IJzendoorn, 1988); and more frequent and more positively toned interactions during social play (Roggman et al., 1987).

In addition, the predictive validity of infant attachment classifications is supported by longitudinal studies of social and emotional development across the preschool and early school years. Secure attachment has been related to aspects of social functioning at preschool, including positive affect, empathy, and compliance (Main & Weston, 1981; Sroufe et al., 1984; Waters, Wippman, & Sroufe, 1979), to more positive friendships at age 5 (Youngblade & Belsky, 1992), and to easy and coherent expression of affect between parents and children at age 6 (Main et al., 1985).

The predictive validity of the avoidant versus resistant attachment classification is less clear, with differences in social and emotional functioning between the two major types of insecure attachment being smaller and less frequent. Erickson, Sroufe, and Egeland (1985) report, however, that avoidant and resistant preschool children (as defined by infant classification) differ in theoretically meaningful ways on questionnaire and behavioral measures. Specifically, avoidant children obtain high scores on hostility and noncompliance, whereas anxious-resistant children are characterized by low scores on agency and high scores on distractibility.

In summary, there is considerable evidence that infant attachment classification is related to social and emotional functioning in infancy and toddlerhood; a growing body of longitudinal research extends the claim for predictive validity from infancy to the early school years. Criticisms have been leveled, however, at much of the research in this area (Lamb, 1987). First, evidence concerning the link between attachment type and later functioning is equivocal for some outcome measures (measures of exploratory competence and sociability yield strong results, whereas evidence concerning cognitive development is weaker). Second, the limited discriminability of the two types of insecure attachment is seen as problematic. Third, much of the research has been based on vague hypotheses, which state simply that secure children show better adjustment and performance as assessed by multiple measures. Finally, methodological problems sometimes create difficulties of interpretation—for example, many studies claiming to assess the implications of attachment for performance fail to measure both constructs (attachment and performance) on both occasions, precluding inferences about the direction of effects (Lamb, 1987).

It should be briefly noted that the predictive validity of attachment patterns has also been addressed by studies investigating the clinical implications of attachment. These studies provide empirical support for the association between early attachment insecurity and subsequent behavioral problems (Greenberg & Speltz, 1988; Lyons-Ruth, Alpern & Repacholi, 1993). Nevertheless, it is clear that this association is not perfect; the null results obtained by some researchers (e.g., Bates & Bayles, 1988) indicate limits to the robustness of the association, and many factors may mediate the influence of early attachment on the course of later development (Belsky & Nezworski, 1988).

ஐ Applying Attachment Theory to Adults' Close Relationships

Bowlby's (1979) theory of attachment deals primarily with the bonds formed between infants and their caregivers. As researchers into adult attachment have pointed out, however, Bowlby contends that the attachment system plays a vital role throughout the life cycle and that attachment behavior characterizes human beings "from the cradle to the grave" (p. 129). In accordance with this contention, Morris (1982) argues that, because of the primacy and depth of the early attachment relationship between infant and caregiver, this bond is likely to serve as a prototype for later intimate relationships. Morris further suggests that striking parallels exist between anxious attachment and both unwise mate selection and dysfunctional marriage.

The extension of attachment principles beyond infancy and childhood is also supported by theoretical work focusing on the definition and description of attachment bonds. Ainsworth (1989), for example, proposes criteria for attachment relationships throughout the life span. Specifically, she suggests that attachment relationships are a particular type of affectional bond; that is, they are relatively long-lasting ties characterized by a desire to maintain closeness to a partner who is seen as unique as an individual and who is not interchangeable with any other. The distinguishing feature of attachments, in comparison to other affectional bonds, is that the individual obtains or seeks closeness from the relationship that, if found, results in feelings of comfort and security. Note that the key themes in this analysis of attachment relationships are proximity maintenance and felt security, consistent with Bowlby's (1979) views about the goals of attachment behavior.

Similarly, Weiss (1982, 1986, 1991) argues that the central features of infant-mother attachment, as described by Bowlby (1979), suggest three criteria of attachment: First, that the person wants to be with the attachment figure, especially under conditions of stress (proximity seeking); second, that he or she derives comfort and security from the attachment figure (secure base); and third, that he or she protests when the attachment figure becomes or threatens to become unavailable (separation protest). Again, this analysis of attachment bonds is based directly on Bowlby's work; note that Weiss's description of proximity seeking includes the notion of safe haven (turning to the attachment figure for comfort in times of stress) and the separation protest characteristic is often considered by attachment researchers to fall within the broad rubric of proximity seeking.

In his later work, Weiss (1991) identifies other key properties of childhood attachments. These can be summarized as follows: elicitation by threat (when children feel under threat, they turn to attachment figures as a source of security); specificity of attachment figure (once attachment to a particular figure has formed, proximity to that figure provides security that other individuals cannot); inaccessibility to conscious control (attachment feelings continue, despite recognition that an attachment figure has become unavailable); persistence (attachment behavior does not habituate and persists in the absence of reinforcement); and insensitivity to experience with the attachment figure (security is linked to proximity to the attachment figure, even when that figure is neglecting or abusive).

Based on their analyses of the criteria for attachment relationships, Ainsworth (1979) and Weiss (1991) conclude that some adult relationships can be validly regarded as attachments. Relationships between adults and their parents and between patients and therapists are likely to display properties of attachment bonds; some friendships may do likewise (Weiss, 1991). In particular, however, Weiss argues that the criteria for attachment are found in most marital and committed nonmarital romantic relationships; similarly, Ainsworth points to sexual pair bonds as a prime example of adult attachment. These arguments can be seen as laying the foundation for empirical studies of adult attachment.

ᴥ Summary

Until recently, attachment theory focused on the bonds between infants and their primary caregivers. Key influences in this area have been Bowlby's (1969, 1973, 1980) seminal work on attachment and loss, which deals with the processes by which infant-caregiver bonds are formed and broken, and Ainsworth's (1979) observational studies of patterns of infant attachment. Subsequent research has provided considerable support for the role of the caregiver's sensitivity and responsiveness in the development of secure attachment; the extent of stability of infant attachment patterns, however, remains a matter of debate. The application of attachment principles beyond infancy and childhood is supported by recent theoretical analyses of the defining criteria of attachment relationships. These analyses set the stage for the first empirical studies of adult attachment, discussed in the next chapter.

2

&

Early Empirical Studies
of Adult Attachment

As we showed in the previous chapter, theoretical work span-
ning the last decade (Ainsworth, 1989; Weiss, 1982; 1986;
1991) supports the relevance of attachment relationships across
the life span. Nevertheless, it was not until Hazan and Shaver
(1987; Shaver & Hazan, 1988; Shaver, Hazan, & Bradshaw, 1988)
reported their groundbreaking studies of romantic love that the
attachment perspective on adult romantic relationships became
firmly established.

Hazan and Shaver (1987; Shaver & Hazan, 1988; Shaver, Hazan,
& Bradshaw, 1988) present theoretical analyses of love and attachment integrated with new empirical data. Their basic argument is
that romantic love can be conceptualized as an attachment

process. According to this perspective, established relationships between lovers and spouses are attachments, as described by Bowlby (1969, 1973, 1980). That is, these relationships are enduring affectional bonds characterized by complex emotional dynamics. Furthermore, romantic love has biological bases and functions related to the quality of parental health and the provision of care to offspring.

Consistent with the basic tenets of attachment theory, Hazan and Shaver (1987; Shaver & Hazan, 1988; Shaver, Hazan, & Bradshaw, 1988) suggest that early variations in social experience produce relatively enduring differences in relationship styles. Thus romantic love may take on different forms, depending on the individual's attachment history. More specifically, Hazan and Shaver argue that the three major attachment styles described in the infant literature (secure, avoidant, and anxious-ambivalent) are manifested in adult romantic love.

✎ Theoretical Analysis of Love as Attachment

Hazan and Shaver's theoretical analysis of romantic love (Shaver & Hazan, 1988) addresses four main issues: the nature of love as an emotion, the relationship between love and attachment, the concept of love as the integration of behavioral systems, and comparison of the attachment perspective with previous conceptualizations of love. We will briefly discuss each of these issues, which provide the background to Hazan and Shaver's empirical studies of adult attachment.

Love as an Emotion

To describe romantic love as an emotion is not to imply that love is "just a feeling." Rather, an emotion is a complex pattern of appraisals and action tendencies (Campos & Barrett, 1984; Frijda, 1986). For each basic emotion, there is a set of typical elicitors or antecedents and a set of typical responses.

In the case of romantic love, possible elicitors include familiarity with the other, having the other satisfy one's own needs, and

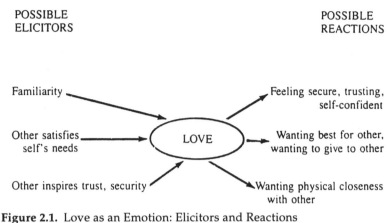

POSSIBLE   POSSIBLE
ELICITORS   REACTIONS

Figure 2.1. Love as an Emotion: Elicitors and Reactions
SOURCE: Shaver and Hazan (1988).

having the other inspire one with trust (see Figure 2.1). Possible reactions include feelings of security and self-confidence, wanting to give to the other, and wanting physical closeness to the other (Shaver & Hazan, 1988). These proposed reactions to the emotion of love (felt security, proximity maintenance) are consistent with the goals of attachment behavior, as defined by Bowlby (1969, 1973, 1980; see Chapter 1 of this volume).

The Relationship Between Love and Attachment

Proposing an association between infant attachment and adult romantic love, Shaver and Hazan (1988; Shaver et al., 1988) tabulate a number of features that show strong parallels across the two types of relationships. Behavioral and emotional similarities include frequent eye contact, smiling, and holding; the desire to share discoveries and reactions with the other; powerful empathy; and so on.

There are also strong parallels between infant-caregiver attachments and romantic love in terms of the dynamics of these relationships. In each case, if the attachment figure is available and responsive, the individual feels secure; if the attachment figure is unavailable, the individual will signal or move closer until feelings of security are restored (refer to the representation of the attachment system in Figure 1.1).

The parallels between the features of infant attachments and romantic love suggest that these two types of relationships may be variants of a single underlying process (Shaver et al., 1988). Note that this theoretical analysis, although more detailed, is similar in focus to the work of Weiss (1982, 1986, 1991) and Ainsworth (1989), who examine the applicability of attachment criteria to adult relationships.

Love as the Integration of Behavioral Systems

Despite their emphasis on the similarities between infant and adult attachments, Shaver and Hazan (1988) clearly recognize that these two types of bonds differ in fundamental ways. Specifically, romantic love (or at least prototypical romantic love) is characterized by reciprocal caregiving, in which each partner moves between the roles of provider and recipient of care (physical, emotional, and material) depending on needs and circumstances. By contrast, infant-caregiver relationships are highly asymmetrical, as the very term *caregiver* implies. In addition, adult romantic love almost always involves a component of sexuality; infants, on the other hand, have a very limited capacity for sexual response.

Hence, Shaver and Hazan (1988) propose that romantic love involves the integration of three behavioral systems: attachment, caregiving, and sexuality. As we saw earlier, Bowlby (1969, 1973, 1980) argues that a number of interlocking behavioral systems, including attachment, caregiving, and sexual mating, serve to ensure the survival of the species.) These three systems are likely to vary in importance across the life cycle of a relationship; for example, sexual attraction and passion tend to be especially strong in the early phases; moreover, the three aspects may vary in importance in different love relationships (Shaver & Hazan, 1988; Shaver et al., 1988). Of the three systems, the attachment system is seen as pivotal; it is the first system to appear in the course of the individual's development, it plays a key role in the formation of mental models of self and others, and hence it lays the foundations for the other systems.

Comparing the Attachment Perspective
With Previous Conceptualizations of Love

In an attempt to integrate theories of love, Shaver and Hazan (1988) compare the attachment perspective with three previous conceptualizations: theories of "anxious love," theories delineating the components of love, and the theory of "love styles." The aim of Shaver and Hazan's analysis is to show that, in comparison with previous accounts, the attachment perspective offers a more comprehensive and theoretically grounded approach to the study of love.

Anxious love. Theories of anxious love, as the name implies, focus on love marked by anxiety, jealousy, obsessiveness, and fear of abandonment. Different researchers and writers have coined different names for anxious love, including *lovesickness* (Hindy & Schwartz, 1985; Money, 1980), *limerence* (Tennov, 1979), and *desperate love* (Sperling, 1985). Shaver and Hazan propose that these forms of love are equivalent to the anxious-ambivalent style of attachment.

If this is so, it appears that researchers have tended to overemphasize anxious love at the expense of other relationship styles; this overemphasis can probably be attributed to the dramatic nature of accounts of anxious love. An equally important criticism of accounts of anxious love is that they have been largely atheoretical; in particular, they have made little attempt to explain the origins of this type of love. Attachment theory, on the other hand, hypothesizes that the anxious-ambivalent relationship style develops as a response to inconsistent or intrusive parenting (although some secure individuals may also display characteristics of anxious love during the early, uncertain, phase of romantic attraction; Shaver & Hazan, 1988).

Componential theories of love

As an example of theories delineating the components of love, Shaver and Hazan (1988) focus on Sternberg's (1986) triangular theory of love. According to this theory, love can be described in terms of three components: intimacy (feelings of closeness and connectedness), passion (drives that lead to physical and sexual attraction), and decision-commitment (the short-term decision that one loves the other and the long-term commitment to maintain that love).

The analogy of the triangle begins with the idea that the three components of love form the vertexes of a triangle. Just as different triangles have different angles, different types of love involve different weightings of the three components (in other words, the relative importance of the three components varies across love relationships). For example, Sternberg sees companionate love as involving an emphasis on intimacy and commitment, but not on passion. In addition, within a single love relationship, the relative importance of the three components may change over time; these changes can also be represented using the analogy of the triangle.

According to Shaver and Hazan (1988), the triangular theory of love is an advance over theories of anxious love insofar as it offers a more complex view of the nature and development of romantic relationships. Nevertheless, the theory is open to criticism; such criticism centers on the choice of components (e.g., little attention is paid to the role of caregiving in love) and on the failure to explain the origins of different forms of love.

Love styles. Finally, Shaver and Hazan (1988) compare the attachment perspective with Lee's (1973, 1988) theory of love styles. Based on detailed interview accounts of adults' love relationships, Lee proposes a typology of love founded on a "color wheel" analogy. According to this typology, there are three primary love styles and three secondary love styles (see Figure 2.2). The three primary love styles are eros (romantic, passionate love), ludus (game-playing love), and storge (friendship love). These primary styles can be combined to form the secondary styles, or compounds: mania (possessive, dependent love; a fusion of eros and ludus); pragma (logical, "shopping-list" love; a fusion of ludus and storge), and agape (selfless, all-giving love; a fusion of storge and eros). The notion of compounds implies that the new styles have quite different properties from either of the component elements. By contrast, the primary styles can also be combined to form mixtures (e.g., storgic-eros) in which the properties of the component elements remain apparent.

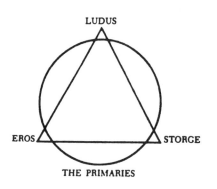

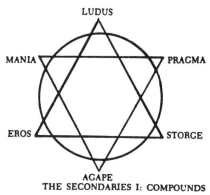

Figure 2.2. Typology of Love Styles
SOURCE: Lee (1973).

Perhaps the most problematic aspect of this theory of love is the analogy of compounds; it is hard to justify regarding mania as a combination of eros and ludus, for example, given that it shows none of the properties of these primary styles. At a broader level, Shaver and Hazan (1988) propose that the typology described within the theory of love styles is essentially reducible to the three major attachment styles. According to this analysis, secure attachment corresponds to a combination of eros and agape, avoidant attachment corresponds to ludus, and anxious-ambivalent attachment corresponds to mania; the remaining love styles (pragma and storge) are discounted as forms of romantic love. We consider empirical evidence for these claims later in this chapter.

Advantages of the attachment perspective. Important advantages of the attachment theoretical approach are noted by Shaver and Hazan (1988) and acknowledged by others (e.g., Clark & Reis, 1988). Three major contributions are as follows. First, the attachment framework provides a developmental perspective: Differing orientations to romantic love are seen as originating in early social experiences, and the mediating processes involving mental models of attachment can account for both the continuity of early relational patterns and the possibility of change. Thus, romantic love is seen not as an isolated phenomenon but as an integral part of human affectional bonding. Second, the theory is sufficiently broad to encompass a range of relationship issues such as love, anxiety, loneliness, and grief. That is, attachment theory deals with issues related to the experience of love; these include the effect of love relationships on other personal relationships and on work projects, and the effects of separation and loss. Third, the attachment perspective is a parsimonious one that enables both healthy and unhealthy forms of love to be explained in terms of the same general principles; the various forms of love are seen as originating as predictable adaptations to specific social circumstances.

❧ The First Empirical Studies of Love as Attachment

Initial empirical support for the attachment perspective on romantic love consisted of two questionnaire-based studies of adult samples (Hazan & Shaver, 1987) investigating the association between attachment style and aspects of childhood and adult relationships. For these studies, Hazan and Shaver developed a forced-choice, self-report measure of adult attachment style. This measure consisted of three short paragraphs, one for each attachment style, with the item content based on extrapolation from the infant literature (see Table 2.1); subjects were asked to choose the paragraph most descriptive of their feelings in close relationships.

Note that Hazan and Shaver's (1987) measure of attachment style was, by necessity, exploratory; the aim, given the available information concerning the characteristics of secure, avoidant, and anxious-ambivalent infants and assuming substantial continuity in these attachment styles, was to capture the main features typifying the three types of adult lovers. In this measure, secure subjects are described as being comfortable with intimacy and able to trust and depend on other people. Avoidant subjects are described as experiencing discomfort with closeness and difficulty in depending on others. Anxious-ambivalent subjects report seeking extreme levels of closeness and fearing that they will be abandoned or not loved sufficiently.

This measure was used in two studies of adult samples (Hazan & Shaver, 1987). The first sample was large (N = 620) and broadly based, consisting of respondents to a "love quiz" presented in a

Table 2.1 Forced-Choice Measure of Attachment Style

Question: Which of the following best describes your feelings?

Secure: I find it relatively easy to get close to others and am comfortable depending on them and having them depend on me. I don't often worry about being abandoned or about someone getting too close to me.

Avoidant: I am somewhat uncomfortable being close to others; I find it difficult to trust them completely, difficult to allow myself to depend on them. I am nervous when anyone gets too close, and love partners often want me to be more intimate than I feel comfortable being.

Anxious-ambivalent: I find that others are reluctant to get as close as I would like. I often worry that my partner doesn't really love me or won't want to stay with me. I want to merge completely with another person, and this desire sometimes scares people away.

SOURCE: Hazan and Shaver (1987).

local newspaper; the second was a sample of undergraduate students. Subjects in both samples completed measures that tapped general attitudes to close relationships, together with specific relationship experiences within their "most important romance."

Results of Hazan and Shaver's (1987) two studies indicate that the relative frequencies of the three styles, as assessed by the forced-choice measure, closely approximate those observed among infants. That is, just over half the subjects classified themselves as secure (56% in each sample); of the remainder, slightly more described themselves as avoidant (23% and 25% in Samples 1 and 2, respectively) than as anxious-ambivalent (20% and 19%, respectively).

In addition, persons endorsing the different attachment styles differed in attachment history (perceptions of early family relationships), endorsement of items designed to tap mental models concerning the self and relationships, and reports of romantic love experiences. The specific pattern of group differences on these measures, as described below and in Table 2.2, was consistent with predictions based on attachment theory.

In comparison with other attachment styles, subjects endorsing the secure description reported warmer childhood relationships with both parents and between their two parents. They saw them-

Table 2.2 Attachment Style Differences on Measures of Attachment History, Mental Models, and Love Experiences

Measure	Secure	Avoidant	Anxious-Ambivalent
Attachment history	Warm relationships with both parents and between the parents	Mothers perceived as cold and rejecting	Fathers perceived as unfair
Mental models	Easy to know; few self-doubts; others well-intentioned; romantic love lasts	Romantic love rarely lasts; romantic love loses intensity	Self-doubts; misunderstood by others; easy to fall in love, but real love rare; others unwilling to commit
Love experiences	Happiness; friendship; trust	Fear of intimacy; difficulty in accepting partner	Obsession and jealousy; desire for union and reciprocation; strong sexual attraction; emotional extremes

selves as easy to get to know and as having few self-doubts and saw other people as well-intentioned. They also believed that romantic love exists in real life and that it does not fade with time. Their most important romantic love relationships were described as relatively happy, friendly, and trusting.

Subjects endorsing the avoidant description were likely to perceive their mothers as cold and rejecting. They were more likely than members of the other attachment groups to question the enduring nature of romantic love. Their most important love experiences were marked by fear of intimacy and by difficulty in accepting their love partners.

Subjects describing themselves as anxious-ambivalent tended to report that their fathers were unfair. They saw themselves as misunderstood by others and as having more self-doubts. They reported that it was easy to fall in love but that they rarely found real love; they also believed that few people were as willing as themselves to commit to a long-term relationship. Their most important love relationships were characterized by obsession and jealousy, desire for union and reciprocation, strong sexual attraction, and emotional extremes.

In reporting these results, Hazan and Shaver (1987) note a number of limitations of their initial empirical studies. Because of the constraints on data collection, for example, many of the measures were brief and involved very simple response alternatives. More important, subjects were asked to describe their experience of a single romantic relationship. Hence, the focus was on relationship qualities that differentiate the three attachment groups. Although this focus on individual differences might be seen as implying a traitlike approach to the construct of attachment style, Hazan and Shaver recognize that relationship qualities are likely to be influenced not only by the individual's attachment style but also by "factors unique to particular partners and circumstances" (p. 521).

In attempting to explain the nature and function of romantic love, Hazan and Shaver (1987) provide a normative account of love relationships; that is, an account of the typical processes of adult romantic attachments. An equally important contribution, however, is to lay the foundations for an understanding of individual differences in adult relationship styles. Their conceptualization of attachment styles enabled a bridge to be built between infant attachment theory and theories of romantic love and generated intense interest among adult relationship researchers.

✿ Early Studies of Adult Attachment: Replicating and Extending the Work of Hazan and Shaver

Hazan and Shaver's initial papers (1987; Shaver & Hazan, 1988) were soon followed by a number of studies reporting replications and extensions of their findings. Most of these early studies of adult attachment made some attempt to address the limitations noted by Hazan and Shaver, thus making advances in conceptualization and measurement; these advances are addressed in more detail in the next chapter. In the rest of this chapter, we focus on the ways in which these early studies provided general support for the attachment perspective on romantic love, either in terms of replicating Hazan and Shaver's findings or in terms of supporting associated theoretical concepts. The studies discussed here are theory-based, in that they deal with key concepts within attachment theory; nevertheless, much of this work has a descriptive flavor, with researchers focusing on clarifying the characteristics of romantic love as it is experienced by the different attachment groups. As we shall point out, however, each of these studies has made some unique contribution to this new research area.

Integrating Theories of Love

The main feature of the first two studies discussed here is their focus on integrating theories of love. Shaver and Hazan (1988) propose that previous conceptualizations of love (theories of anxious love, componential theories of love, and the theory of love styles) can be integrated within the attachment perspective.

Following this proposition, Levy and Davis (1988) assessed the interrelationships between measures of attachment style and the six love styles described by Lee (1973, 1988). (Scales measuring these love styles were developed by Hendrick and Hendrick, 1986 and Hendrick, Hendrick, Foote, & Slapion-Foote, 1984.) Recall that according to Shaver and Hazan (1988), this typology of love styles should be reducible to the three major attachment styles: secure attachment should correspond to a combination of eros and agape; avoidant attachment should correspond to ludus; and anxious-ambivalent attachment should correspond to mania.

Using rating scales to assess each attachment style (see Chapter 3 in this volume), Levy and Davis (1988) report modest correlations between various love styles and attachment styles, lending substantial support to Shaver and Hazan's (1988) formulation: Secure attachment was related positively to eros and agape and negatively to ludus; avoidant attachment was related positively to ludus and negatively to eros; and anxious-ambivalent attachment was related positively to mania. Note that the pattern of relations predicted by Levy and Davis differs slightly from that proposed by Shaver and Hazan; in particular, Levy and Davis argue that secure attachment should be related to storge (an association that failed to emerge).

Levy and Davis (1988) also assessed the links between attachment styles and measures of the three components of love in Sternberg's (1986) model: intimacy, passion, and commitment. They found that all three components of love were related positively to secure attachment and negatively to avoidant and anxious-ambivalent attachment. Although Shaver and Hazan (1988) do not specify the expected links between these two sets of measures, Levy and Davis's results support the link between secure attachment and relationship quality. The fact that the two forms of insecure attachment showed similar links with all components of love might appear problematic because one would expect each attachment style to have a unique set of correlates. (Recall the studies of predictive validity of infant attachment styles, reported in Chapter 1, and showing limited discriminability of the two forms of insecure attachment.) Other measures employed by Levy and Davis did support the distinction between avoidant and anxious-ambivalent attachment, however: They found that avoidance was more strongly associated with lack of commitment to romantic relationships and anxious-ambivalence-was associated with a dominating style of response to conflict.

Research reported by Feeney and Noller (1990) has two major aims: first, to replicate Hazan and Shaver's (1987) findings linking adult attachment style with early family history and with mental models of attachment, and second, to address unresolved issues concerning the proposed integration of theories of love. Using a large sample of university students, Feeney and Noller report attachment group differences on measures of early family history and mental models of relationships that largely support the earlier work. A noteworthy finding to emerge from this study is that avoidant subjects were more likely than others to report having experienced a lengthy period of separation from their mothers during childhood. This finding is consistent with the principles of attachment theory, although Hazan and Shaver (1987) did not find a significant link between adult attachment style and episodes of separation from parents during childhood.

Like Levy and Davis (1988), Feeney and Noller (1990) were also interested in how the attachment perspective related to previous theories of love. Specifically, Feeney and Noller saw a need to clarify two aspects of the links proposed by Shaver and Hazan (1988). The first of these concerns the role of storge (friendship love). Shaver and Hazan argue that storge is "not a romantic style at all," whereas Levy and Davis hypothesize a link between storge and secure attachment but fail to support this link. Second, the relation between forms of anxious love and anxious-ambivalent attachment received little empirical attention. Shaver and Hazan describe theories of anxious love as unidimensional; however, they did not test whether constructs such as limerence are, in fact, unidimensional, and whether they are largely redundant with anxious-ambivalent attachment.

For these reasons, Feeney and Noller (1990) explore attachment group differences in relationship experiences using a broad range of relevant variables: self-esteem, loving (defined by using Rubin's, 1973, Love Scale), love styles (using Hendrick & Hendrick's, 1986, items), limerence (love marked by fear of rejection, emotional extremes, and preoccupation, as discussed by Tennov, 1979), and love addiction (involving obsession, overinvolvement, and extreme dependency, as discussed by Peele, 1975, 1988). The structure of each measure was investigated using factor analysis, which resulted in 16 scales. Two points of interest emerged here. First, although the measure of love styles revealed six major factors, these did not correspond exactly to the six scales described by Hendrick and Hendrick (1986). For example, a friendship factor was obtained that consisted of five items from the storge scale and two from the eros scale (both focusing on gradual involvement in relationships). Second, there was evidence that most measures of anxious love involve more than one dimension. The 42-item limerence measure, for example, seemed to tap four different aspects of anxious love: obsessive preoccupation, self-conscious anxiety, emotional dependence, and idealization.

Second-order factor analysis of the 16 scales used in Feeney and Noller's (1990) study provides an integration of the key themes present in previous measures of love. Four factors were revealed: neurotic love (involving obsessive preoccupation, emotional dependence, and idealization of the partner), self-confidence (high self-esteem, together with lack of self-conscious anxiety in dealing with romantic partners), avoidance of intimacy (high scores on ludus and low scores on items related to loving, eros, and agape), and circumspect love (friendship and pragma).

Differences between attachment groups were obtained for all four of these second-order scales, clarifying the links between attachment style and other theories of love. Secure subjects obtained high scores on self-confidence and low scores on the three remaining scales (neurotic love, avoidance of intimacy, and circumspect love). Both insecure groups reported low self-confidence, but clearly differed in other respects. As would be expected, avoidant subjects were marked by avoidance of intimacy. By contrast, anxious-ambivalent subjects obtained high scores on neurotic love and low scores on circumspect love. These results generally support Shaver and Hazan's (1988) theoretical formulation, but point to some important qualifications. In particular, although Shaver and Hazan equate limerence with anxious-ambivalent attachment, it appears that limerence has several components and that one of these (self-conscious anxiety in dealing with romantic partners) characterizes both avoidant and anxious-ambivalent individuals.

In summary, the studies outlined in this section suggest that the attachment perspective offers an integrative view of romantic love. Attachment theory appears to encompass the major variables discussed in previous theories of love; specifically, attachment style is related in meaningful ways to measures of anxious love, the various love styles, and the components of love relationships. Nevertheless, the limited overlap between attachment style and these measures, together with the complex nature of constructs such as limerence, caution against a simplistic model that equates particular attachment styles with other forms of love.

Adult Attachment Styles and Affect Regulation

In Chapter 1, we state that attachment theory can be described as a theory of affect regulation; that is, a theory about how people handle negative emotion. Individual differences in attachment style are thought to develop from infants' experiences of regulating distress with caregivers. In other words, based on the caregiver's responsiveness to the infant's signals of distress, the infant learns a set of strategies for organizing emotional experience and dealing with negative feelings (Sroufe & Waters, 1977). By the process of generalization, these strategies come to be applied to any distressing situation. Strategies learned through interactions with caregivers are adaptive, in the sense of meeting the infant's short-term goals; however, they may be either appropriate or inappropriate for dealing with situations in the longer term.

Similarly, adult attachment styles should be associated with characteristic patterns of response to distress. Secure individuals should handle negative feelings in a relatively constructive manner by acknowledging their distress and turning to others for support and comfort; these strategies stem from their experiences of responsive caregiving. Avoidant individuals are likely to show restricted acknowledgment of negative feelings and restricted displays of anger and distress, learned as a strategy for reducing conflict with rejecting or insensitive caregivers. A highly self-reliant approach is thus adopted at the expense of seeking others' support. Anxious-ambivalent individuals are likely to show relatively constant awareness of negative feelings. They focus their attention on these feelings in a hypervigilant way and display heightened expressions of fear and anger; these strategies have been learned as a way of maintaining contact with inconsistent caregivers (Kobak & Sceery, 1988).

A number of early studies of adult attachment explored the link between attachment patterns and affect regulation. Kobak and Sceery (1988) examined attachment style, representations of self and others, and affect regulation using a sample of first-year college students. Based on interviews assessing subjects' relationships with their parents, subjects were classified as secure, dismissing of attachment (cf. avoidant), or preoccupied (cf. anxious-ambivalent). Representations of self and others were measured using self-report scales (distress, social competence, and social support) and affect regulation was measured using peer Q-sort ratings of ego resilience (social skill, warmth, insight into self), ego undercontrol (changeability, self-indulgence, rebel-

lion), hostility (including blame and criticism), and anxiety (intro-
spection, need for reassurance, fear, and guilt).

As expected, secure subjects showed constructive ways of handling negative feelings in social contexts: They were seen by peers
as more ego resilient, less anxious, and less hostile and reported
high levels of social support and little distress. By contrast, both
groups of insecure subjects were rated by peers as low on ego
resilience. Dismissing subjects were also rated by peers as high on
hostility, but reported similar levels of social competence and
distress as secure subjects; together, these findings suggest a possible failure by these individuals to acknowledge their negative
feelings. Preoccupied subjects were seen by peers as high in
anxiety and reported high levels of distress; these results are
consistent with the proposition that anxious-ambivalent individuals show both heightened awareness and heightened expression of negative feelings.

As noted earlier, the rules that infants learn about regulating
attachment-related distress are thought to generalize to other distressing situations. Pursuing this argument, Mikulincer, Florian,
and Tolmacz (1990) studied attachment and affect regulation in the
context of the fear of personal death. These researchers argue that
fear of death is a universal fear that involves separation from loved
persons and hence is likely to activate attachment-related
schemas.

Using an instrument derived from Hazan and Shaver's (1987)
measure of attachment style, Mikulincer et al. (1990) classified
subjects as secure, avoidant, or anxious-ambivalent; self-report
and projective measures were used to assess the extent of fear of
personal death and the motives for such fear. Attachment style was
related to the extent of fear of death and to the motives for fear.
Secure subjects generally experienced less fear of death than insecure subjects. Avoidant subjects were likely to fear the unknown
nature of death, whereas anxious-ambivalent subjects were likely
to fear the loss of social identity in death. These links between
forms of insecure attachment and motives for fear of death were
not exactly as hypothesized and are open to alternative explanations; nevertheless, findings from this study suggest that attach-

ment group differences in affect regulation are worthy of further study.

The association between attachment style and the regulation of negative affect *within* romantic relationships is explored by Simpson (1990). Heeding Hazan and Shaver's (1987) call for attachment researchers to study both partners in ongoing relationships, Simpson employed a sample of dating couples. He was interested in the link between attachment style and reports of emotional experience, both in terms of the emotional quality of the relationship itself and in terms of responses to relationship breakup. The emotional quality of the current relationship was assessed by asking subjects how often within that relationship they experienced each of 28 different emotions. These emotions represented four categories: mild positive, intense positive, mild negative, and intense negative. Secure subjects reported more frequent positive emotions and less frequent negative emotions (both mild and intense) than did avoidant and anxious-ambivalent subjects. This finding may reflect two interrelated effects: Secure subjects may form relationships of high quality and may be better able to perceive and interpret relationship events in a positive way.

Responses to relationship breakup were assessed at a 6-month follow-up by surveying couples who were no longer together. This survey focused on the extent of emotional distress experienced following the breakup. Consistent with theory linking attachment style and affect regulation, avoidant attachment was associated with less postdissolution distress, although this effect was obtained only for men. Simpson's (1990) results are also partially consistent with other research relating attachment style to reports of emotional responses to relationship dissolution (Feeney & Noller, 1992). Feeney and Noller (1992) found that, although secure attachment was unrelated to reports of emotional response, avoidant attachment was correlated negatively with upset and positively with relief, whereas anxious-ambivalent attachment was correlated positively with surprise and upset and negatively with relief.

Relationship Functioning

Simpson (1990) was also interested in the quality of dating relationships as reported by the different attachment groups. Results point to the link between secure attachment and high levels of trust, commitment, satisfaction, and interdependence (i.e., love, dependence, and self-disclosure). By contrast, both avoidant and anxious-ambivalent attachment were negatively related to trust and satisfaction and avoidant attachment was also linked with low levels of interdependence and commitment. These results are largely consistent with attachment theory. They also fit with the findings of Levy and Davis (1988), as described in the section on integrating theories of love.

Another important study of relationship functioning in dating couples was conducted by Collins and Read (1990). (This study also addressed key issues concerning the conceptualization and measurement of adult attachment and the role of working models; these issues are discussed in Chapters 3 and 6 in this volume.) Collins and Read measured attachment style using three scales: close (assessing comfort with closeness), depend (assessing trust and the extent to which others are seen as available and dependable), and anxiety (assessing anxiety over relationship issues, such as being unloved). In terms of the three-group measure of attachment style, secure and anxious-ambivalent subjects obtained higher scores on close and depend than did avoidant subjects; anxious-ambivalent subjects reported more anxiety over relationships than the secure and avoidant groups.

The implications of attachment dimensions for relationship quality were largely gender specific. For females, anxiety over relationship issues was a strong correlate of reported relationship quality. Specifically, the anxiety scale was linked with jealousy and with low levels of satisfaction, perceived closeness to partner, trust in partner, partner responsiveness, and communication. For males, relationship quality was related strongly to comfort with closeness; this variable was associated with high levels of satisfaction, perceived closeness to partner, liking of partner, likelihood of marrying partner, trust in partner, communication, and self-disclosure. Despite this overall pattern of gender differences, some findings were robust across gender: For example, both men and women who were comfortable with closeness reported being able to get other people to open up and talk about personal information, and men and women who were anxious about relationships reported a lack of trust in their partners.

The studies reported in this section employed both members of dating couples. This feature allowed the researchers to assess whether perceptions of relationship functioning were related to partners' attachment style as well as to subjects' attachment style. This issue is addressed in some detail in the next chapter; briefly, the results of these studies suggest that, on average, individuals with secure partners report better relationship functioning than those with insecure partners. As we discuss next, another approach to exploring the issue of relationship functioning was also soon adopted; this approach involves using less structured assessment tools to explore the implications of subjects' own attachment style. This research provides convergent evidence for attachment group differences in relationship quality.

Open-Ended Reports of Attachment-Related Issues

All the studies reported so far support the association between adult attachment style and the quality of romantic relationships. It should be noted, however, that these studies relied primarily on a closed-ended, self-report method of data collection. Even the study by Kobak and Sceery (1988), which supplemented this method with peer reports and interviews, employed measures in which the experimenters provided the structure. Reliance on such measures leaves some important methodological issues unresolved. Highly structured psychological measures, especially closed-ended questionnaires, may lead to response sets such as social desirability and experimenter demand. Feeney and Noller (1991) suggest that, although early measures of adult attachment have proved to be strong predictors of relationship quality, the issues raised in these measures may not be important to subjects' evaluations of their romantic relationships except when they are introduced by the measurement procedure. In particular, questionnaire-based studies do not establish the *salience* of attachment-related issues to subjects' evaluations of their relationships.

In an attempt to address this problem, Feeney and Noller (1991) conducted a study in which subjects who were currently in dating relationships provided open-ended verbal descriptions of their relationships. Subjects were asked to speak for 5 minutes, telling "what kind of person your partner is, and how you get along together." The descriptions were audiotaped and later transcribed for content analysis. Two weeks after this procedure, subjects completed the measure of attachment style developed by Hazan and Shaver (1987); the measures were obtained in this order to prevent the questionnaire measure from contaminating the content of the unstructured verbal descriptions.

These data enabled Feeney and Noller (1991) to address two main questions. First, they assessed the salience of attachment-related issues by examining the frequency of subjects' spontaneous references to these issues. They defined five attachment-related issues: openness, closeness, dependence, commitment, and affection. The first four of these issues were chosen to capture the key aspects of mental models of attachment; previous work indicates that avoidant subjects are differentiated from secure subjects by their low levels of trust and expressiveness and by their avoidance of closeness, and that anxious-ambivalent subjects are characterized by dependence and the search for commitment (Feeney & Noller, 1990; Hazan & Shaver, 1987). The fifth issue, affection, was chosen because of its centrality to attachment theory, which deals with the formation and expression of bonds of affection.

For each issue, Feeney and Noller (1990) coded content according to the categories shown in Table 2.3. Each attachment-related issue was spontaneously mentioned by at least 25% of subjects, with 89% of the subject sample referring to at least one of the five issues. The salience of attachment-related issues was further supported by the finding that, in terms of word counts, one fifth of the content of transcripts was devoted to discussion of these issues.

The second question addressed by Feeney and Noller (1990) concerns the link between attachment style (as assessed by Hazan and Shaver's, 1987, measure) and open-ended reports of relationship quality. Secure, avoidant, and anxious-ambivalent subjects

Table 2.3 Coding of Attachment-Related Issues

Issue	Content	Categories	Examples
Openness	References to open expression of thoughts, feelings	Seen as desirable Not mentioned	She's very open with me, which is good
Closeness	Attitudes to closeness, intimacy	Limits advocated Unqualified desire for Not mentioned	He doesn't want too much closeness, which is good We're about as close as a couple can get
Dependence	Attitudes to dependence, possessiveness, sharing of time and activities	Limits advocated Unqualified desire for Not mentioned	She is too dependent; more clingy than I am If we spend more than a day apart, I go haywire
Commitment	Attitudes to commitment, seriousness of relationship	Limits advocated Unqualified desire for Not mentioned	She pressures me for more commitment than I want I'm much more likely than she is to get heavily committed
Affection	Attitudes to the expression of love and affection	Limits advocated Unqualified desire for Not mentioned	I wouldn't want someone who "loves you, loves you" all the time All my life I've craved this sort of affection

SOURCE: Feeney and Noller (1991).

clearly differed in the content of their reports, as indicated by analyses comparing these groups in terms of their references to attachment-related issues and to other themes emerging from the transcripts. The major features of the three groups are illustrated by the three extracts shown in Table 2.4, which were supplied by young women of different attachment styles.

Table 2.4 Extracts From Open-Ended Reports of Romantic
Relationships Supplied by Subjects From the Three
Attachment Groups

Secure: We're really good friends, and we sort of knew each other for a long
time before we started going out—and we like the same sort of things. Another
thing which I like a lot is that he gets on well with all my close friends. We can
always talk things over. Like if we're having any fights, we usually resolve them
by talking it over—he's a very reasonable person. I can just be my own person,
so it's good, because it's not a possessive relationship. I think that we trust each
other a lot.

Avoidant: My partner is my best friend, and that's the way I think of him. He's
as special to me as any of my other friends. His expectations in life don't include
marriage, or any long-term commitment to any female, which is fine with me,
because that's not what my expectations are as well. I find that he doesn't want
to be overly intimate, and he doesn't expect too much commitment—which is
good. . . . We're very close—it's a kind of a comfort, but sometimes it's a
worry—that a person can be that close to you, and be in such control of your life.

Anxious-Ambivalent: So I went in there. . .and he was sitting on the bench, and
I took one look, and I actually melted. He was the best-looking thing I'd ever
seen, and that was the first thing that struck me about him. So we went out and
we had lunch in the park. . . . so we just sort of sat there—and in silence—but it
wasn't awkward. . .like, you know, when you meet strangers and you can't think
of anything to say, it's usually awkward. It wasn't like that. We just sat there,
and it was incredible—like we'd known each other for a real long time, and we'd
only met for about 10 seconds, so that was—straightaway my first feelings for
him started coming out.

SOURCE: Feeney and Noller (1991).

Secure subjects emphasized relationship closeness but also advocated a balance in terms of the extent to which partners depend
on each other; they also made relatively frequent references to
partners' mutual support and encouragement. Both secure and
avoidant subjects tended to describe their relationships as involving friendship; unlike secure subjects, however, those who
described themselves as avoidant preferred clear limits to closeness, dependence, commitment, and the expression of affection.
By contrast, anxious-ambivalent subjects preferred unqualified
closeness, commitment, and affection in their relationships; they
also tended to idealize their partners. These results fit neatly with
the principles of attachment theory and with empirical analyses

relating attachment style to more structured measures of relationship quality.

ა Summary

Hazan and Shaver's (1987; Shaver and Hazan, 1988; Shaver et al., 1988) initial papers on adult attachment provide a substantial body of theoretical and empirical evidence for the attachment perspective on romantic love. Early studies by other adult attachment researchers provide further support, particularly with regard to integrating theories of love and describing attachment group differences in affect regulation and relationship quality. Open-ended verbal reports establish that individuals spontaneously refer to attachment-related issues in describing their dating relationships; moreover, the specific content of these descriptions is consistent with the key features of the various attachment groups. Despite the promising results of these early studies, major issues concerning the conceptualization and measurement of adult attachment style are surfacing in the literature. These issues are addressed in the next chapter.

3

❦

Conceptualizing and Measuring Adult Attachment

Hazan and Shaver's (1987) studies of adult attachment provided the impetus for what soon became a burgeoning field of research. As Hazan and Shaver and other researchers point out, however, the original forced-choice item (see Table 2.1) clearly had limitations as a measure of attachment style. In particular, reliance on a single item raised concerns about the reliability of measurement. These concerns were exacerbated by the fact that the forced-choice format requires subjects to choose from complex alternatives, each covering a range of themes (e.g., trust, dependence, and comfort with closeness).

In discussing attachment measures, three points should be noted. First, despite the calls for more refined instruments, Hazan and Shaver's (1987) categorical measure remains reasonably popular. Several factors may account for this popularity. Measures that clearly emphasize individual differences in relationship experiences seem to have intuitive appeal, as do simple typologies; moreover, because this measure is based on findings from the infant literature, parallels can be drawn between adult relationship styles and the major infant attachment styles. A further advantage lies in the fact that the measure is quick and easy to administer.

Second, researchers have tended to focus on the reliability of attachment measures, particularly in terms of stability over time. This focus on reliability is not without foundation, because unreliable measures produce unstable results that cannot be replicated; moreover, attachment theory assumes a certain amount of continuity in attachment patterns. At the same time, it is widely acknowledged that even the simplest attachment measures show consistent associations with relationship variables and hence must possess a fair degree of reliability and validity. The question then is not whether the early measures of adult attachment are capable of producing meaningful results, but rather how these measures might be improved psychometrically.

Finally, it is important to note that Hazan and Shaver (1987) were not the first researchers to measure adult attachment. For example, the Adult Attachment Interview (George, Kaplan, & Main, 1985) was designed to tap subjects' memories of their childhood relationships with parents, together with current evaluations of these early experiences and their effects on adult personality. Interview transcripts are used to identify three attachment patterns: secure (marked by ease and objectivity in discussing attachment episodes and by the valuing of attachment experiences), dismissing (marked by difficulty in recalling specific attachment experiences and by the devaluing of attachment relationships), and preoccupied (marked by confused and incoherent accounts of attachment relationships). The validity of this measure is supported by links between parents' attachment patterns, as assessed by the Adult Attachment Interview, and their children's attachment type, as assessed 6 years earlier using the Strange Situation (Main & Goldwyn, 1985). One disadvantage of the Adult Attachment Interview is that administration and scoring require in-depth training. For this reason, researchers have sought simpler and more economical means of assessing adult attachment. In this chapter, we focus on measures following the work of Hazan and Shaver (1987).

❧ Derivatives of Hazan and Shaver's Original Measure

Moving Beyond the Forced-Choice Format

Given researchers' concerns about the utility of Hazan and Shaver's (1987) original measure, alternative versions were soon developed. The first of these involves a relatively minor revision to the format of the measure: The original three descriptions are presented intact, but rather than being forced to choose between them, subjects rate the applicability of each one. Specifically, subjects are asked to indicate the degree to which each description "fits your feelings and experiences in relationships," using Likert-type scales ranging from "not at all" to "completely or almost completely" (Levy & Davis, 1988).

This approach to measurement allows for more complete descriptions of individuals' attachment styles. First, it recognizes that not all subjects choosing a particular attachment style (e.g., secure) will find the associated description equally applicable. That is, some will be more "secure" than others. Second, it allows researchers to consider attachment profiles or patterns of scores across the three styles. Subjects who see themselves as secure, for example, will differ in their degree of avoidance and anxious-ambivalence because attachment styles are unlikely to be mutually exclusive. These patterns of secondary ratings may have important implications for relationship quality and individual adjustment.

Using this revised measure with two adult samples, Levy and Davis (1988) found consistent patterns of correlations among the three styles: Secure and avoidant attachment showed a moderate negative correlation; secure and anxious-ambivalent attachment were negatively but weakly related; and avoidant and anxious-ambivalent attachment showed a near-zero correlation. The substantial association between secure and avoidant attachment revealed by these correlational data is noteworthy and raises important questions about the appropriateness of a theoretical model that proposes three separate types. Such questions, however, are not readily answered using either the forced-choice or the revised measure; because both versions involve subjects responding to the three original descriptions, any unexpected findings may reflect problems with the wording of these descriptions rather than with the underlying theoretical model.

Developing Multiple-Item Attachment Scales

To obtain a more complete understanding of the nature of adult attachment, researchers developed measures that involve more extensive modification of the original single item. The basic approach is to take the three a priori descriptions derived by Hazan and Shaver (1987) and to break each one into a number of statements to which subjects can respond using rating scales. This procedure makes it easier for subjects who have difficulty choosing between the three descriptions. Also, from the researchers' perspective, these measures allow more fine-grained analysis of subjects' attachment concerns. For example, it is no longer assumed that the various themes within each a priori description form a consistent whole; rather, researchers can investigate the underlying structure of attachment measures using empirical methods, such as factor analysis.

Within this basic approach, however, the actual item content varies substantially from measure to measure. Some researchers base their items directly on Hazan and Shaver's (1987) three descriptions (e.g., Feeney, Noller, & Callan, 1994; Mikulincer et al., 1990; Simpson, 1990; Simpson, Rholes, & Nelligan, 1992), but even these researchers do not produce identical measures because the broad descriptions are broken down in slightly different ways. Other researchers omit or add items based on particular theoretical or empirical considerations. For example, Carnelley and Janoff-Bulman (1992) omitted two items that they regarded as ambiguous or as redundant with other items in the set. Collins and Read (1990) added items designed to tap two aspects of attachment that they considered lacking in Hazan and Shaver's measure: confidence in the availability and dependability of others and reactions to separations from the attachment figure.

Because of variations in item content across studies, consensus concerning the major dimensions underlying attachment measures has been rather slow to emerge. As Hazan and Shaver (1994) note, the results of factor analyses clearly depend on the items used; such analyses cannot tell us whether those items adequately represent the domain of interest. Collins and Read (1990), for example, found three factors, one of which included the items on availability and dependability added by these researchers.

Nevertheless, research in this area points to some consistent findings. In particular, results of several studies suggest that when the content of multiple-item measures is based closely on Hazan and Shaver's (1987) descriptions of attachment styles, two major dimensions emerge: comfort with closeness and anxiety over relationships (Feeney, 1994; Feeney, Noller, & Callan, 1994; Griffin & Bartholomew, 1994; Simpson et al., 1992; Strahan, 1991).

Comfort with closeness is a bipolar dimension that essentially contrasts elements of the original secure and avoidant descriptions (e.g., "I find it relatively easy to get close to others," versus "I am nervous when anyone gets too close"). Anxiety over relationships deals with concerns about lack of love and possible abandonment by relationship partners and with the desire for extreme closeness (e.g., "I often worry that my partner doesn't really love me"; "I often worry that my partner won't want to stay with me"; "I find that others are reluctant to get as close as I would like"). This dimension corresponds closely to anxious-ambivalent attachment.

More broadly based multiple-item measures also suggest the importance of these two dimensions. Feeney, Noller, and Hanrahan (1994) developed a large pool of items designed to cover the basic themes of infant and adult attachment theory (trust, dependence, need for approval, compulsive self-reliance, etc.). Factor analysis of the items revealed five main factors: confidence (in self and others), discomfort with closeness, need for approval, preoccupation with relationships, and relationships as secondary to achievement. Distinct groups of individuals were identified using cluster analysis, with the five scales as the clustering variables. These attachment groups were best described in terms of two dimensions: anxiety over relationships (defined by preoccupation with relationships, need for approval, and lack of confidence) and discomfort with closeness (defined by discomfort with closeness and relationships as secondary).

❧ A Four-Group Model of Adult Attachment

At the same time that researchers were assessing the utility of the three-group measure and its various derivatives, theoretical and empirical work was presented proposing a four-group model of adult attachment (Bartholomew, 1990; Bartholomew & Horowitz, 1991). This model was based on Bowlby's (1969, 1973) contention that attachment patterns reflect working models of the self and the attachment figure. According to Bartholomew (1990), models of the self can be dichotomized as either positive (the self is seen as worthy of love and attention) or negative (the self is seen as unworthy). Similarly, models of the attachment figure can be positive (the other is seen as available and caring) or negative (the other is seen as rejecting, distant, or uncaring).

Bartholomew (1990) proposes that the working model of self (positive, negative) can be combined with the working model of other to define four adult attachment styles (see Figure 3.1). Hence, these four styles arise from two underlying dimensions: the object of mental models (self or other) and the predominant feeling about that object (positive or negative). As shown in Figure 3.1, the model of self reflects the extent of dependence on others' acceptance (negative models of the self are associated with dependence) and the model of other reflects the extent of avoidance of close relationships (negative models of others are associated with avoidance).

According to Batholomew's (1990) perspective, individuals with positive models of others (i.e., nonavoidant) may be clas-

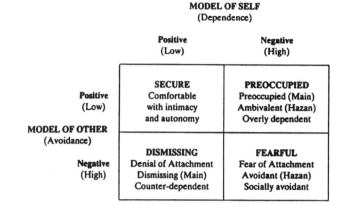

MODEL OF SELF
(Dependence)

		Positive (Low)	Negative (High)
MODEL OF OTHER (Avoidance)	Positive (Low)	**SECURE** Comfortable with intimacy and autonomy	**PREOCCUPIED** Preoccupied (Main) Ambivalent (Hazan) Overly dependent
	Negative (High)	**DISMISSING** Denial of Attachment Dismissing (Main) Counter-dependent	**FEARFUL** Fear of Attachment Avoidant (Hazan) Socially avoidant

Figure 3.1. Four-Group Model of Adult Attachment
SOURCE: Bartholomew (1990).

sified as either secure or preoccupied, depending on their degree of dependence; these styles are similar to Hazan and Shaver's (1987) secure and anxious-ambivalent styles, respectively. Individuals with negative models of others (i.e., avoidant) may be either dismissing or fearful, depending again on the extent of dependence. That is, both dismissing and fearful groups tend to avoid close relationships but differ in their dependence upon others' acceptance. Dismissing avoidants emphasize the importance of achievement and self-reliance; hence they maintain a sense of self-worth at the expense of intimacy. By contrast, fearful avoidants desire intimacy but experience lack of trust and fear of rejection; for this reason, they avoid close relationships in which they may be vulnerable to loss or rejection (Bartholomew, 1990; Bartholomew & Horowitz, 1991). Bartholomew suggests that Hazan and Shaver's avoidant group may correspond to the fearful avoidant style because the description of avoidance in the three-group measure refers explicitly to discomfort with closeness.

Bartholomew and Horowitz (1991) developed prototypical descriptions of the four attachment styles, similar in form to the three attachment descriptions used by Hazan and Shaver (1987; see Table 3.1). As with the three-group measure, these descriptions

Table 3.1 Prototypical Descriptions of Four Attachment Styles

Secure: It is relatively easy for me to become emotionally close to others. I am comfortable depending on others and having others depend on me. I don't worry about being alone or having others not accept me.

Dismissing: I am comfortable without close emotional relationships. It is very important to me to feel independent and self-sufficient, and I prefer not to depend on others or have others depend on me.

Preoccupied: I want to be completely emotionally intimate with others, but I often find that others are reluctant to get as close as I would like. I am uncomfortable being without close relationships, but I sometimes worry that others don't value me as much as I value them.

Fearful: I am somewhat uncomfortable getting close to others. I want emotionally close relationships, but I find it difficult to trust others completely or to depend on them. I sometimes worry that I will be hurt if I allow myself to become too close to others.
Note: Subsequent minor revisions to the above wording are reported by Bartholomew & Horowitz, 1991.

SOURCE: Bartholomew and Horowitz, (1991).

can be presented either in forced-choice format or using rating scales. Interview schedules have also been developed that yield ratings on each of the four prototypes (Bartholomew & Horowitz, 1991).

Empirical data support the utility of the four-group model 1f adult attachment. First, cross-tabulation of Bartholomew's (1991) categorical measure with that developed by Hazan and Shaver (1987) yields theoretically meaningful results (Brennan, Shaver, & Tobey, 1991). As expected, subjects endorsing the secure category of one measure are also likely to endorse the secure category of the other, and those who endorse Bartholomew's preoccupied category are likely to see themselves as anxious-ambivalent in terms of Hazan and Shaver's (1987) measure. Bartholomew's fearful avoidants are drawn largely from Hazan and Shaver's avoidant group, whereas the dismissing avoidants are drawn from both secure and avoidant groups.

Second, there is considerable support for the proposition that two distinct groups of avoidant individuals can be identified. Bartholomew and Horowitz (1991) show that fearful and dismissing avoidants, as defined by attachment interviews, can be differentiated on relevant measures. For example, the interpersonal problems of fearful avoidants involve social insecurity and lack of assertiveness, whereas those of dismissing avoidants involve excessive coldness. Furthermore, Feeney, Noller, and Hanrahan (1994) found that the five attachment scales of their self-report measure could be used to define four distinct attachment groups, which were generally similar to those proposed by Bartholomew (1990). In comparison with dismissing avoidants, fearful avoidants reported less confidence in self and others, more discomfort with closeness, greater need for approval from others, and more preoccupation with relationships.

Given these findings, researchers using a priori attachment descriptions (whether in forced-choice or rating scale format) have increasingly adopted the four-group model. It is interesting to note that the four-group typology is also consistent with research into infant attachment behavior, which suggests the importance of the recent addition of the disorganized-disoriented (D, or A-C) group (see Chapter 1 in this volume). Brennan et al. (1991) suggest that the fearful-avoidant group is analogous to the A-C group in infancy; this proposition receives some indirect support from the fact that fearful avoidants show an attachment profile indicative of extreme insecurity (Feeney, Noller, & Hanrahan, 1994).

❧ Categorical and Continuous Measures Compared

Although researchers have debated the relative merits of categorical and continuous measures, there is evidence that these two approaches yield consistent descriptions of individual differences in attachment. Specifically, it appears that the two key dimensions of comfort with closeness and anxiety over relationships (discussed above) are closely tied to the four groups of Bartholomew's (1990) model. When subjects' responses to forced-choice and continuous measures are compared, comfort with closeness typically separates dismissing and fearful avoidant groups from secure and preoccupied groups, with the avoidant groups obtaining lower mean scores; anxiety over relationships typically separates preoccupied and fearful groups from secure and dismissing groups, with the latter obtaining lower mean scores (Feeney, 1995a; Feeney, Noller, and Hanrahan, 1994).

These results suggest that comfort with closeness is linked with mental models of others, and hence with the extent of social avoidance. Such a link is consistent with the content of items assessing comfort with closeness. Anxiety over relationships appears to be closely linked with mental models of the self, and hence with the extent of dependence. Again, this link fits with the basic theme of anxiety over relationships.

❧ Stability of Adult Attachment

Although empirical research has indicated reasonable stability of attachment security across the childhood years (see Chapter 1), the stability of attachment patterns is still a major issue for developmental researchers. This issue has been equally salient in the context of adult attachment research. Questions about the extent of stability are tied closely to other contentious issues in this area. Most notably, controversy has centered around the "trait versus relationships" debate (which we return to later in this chapter): The issue of whether adult attachment measures are tapping enduring characteristics of individuals or functioning in current relationships.

Assessing the Extent of Stability

Researchers have investigated the stability of adult attachment patterns over intervals ranging from 1 week to 4 years. Stability has been assessed using all forms of measures: forced-choice (both three group and four group), Likert ratings of attachment prototypes, and multiple-item scales. In the following sections, we present empirical evidence concerning the stability of these various measures and then discuss the implications of these findings for the conceptualization of attachment.

Forced-choice measures. Research into the stability of the *three-group* forced-choice measure is summarized in Table 3.2. The most comprehensive report is provided by Baldwin and Fehr (1995).

Table 3.2 Stability of the Three-Group Forced-Choice Measure of Adult
Attachment

		Degree (%) of Stability			
Sample	Timelag	Time 1 Secure	Time 1 Avoidant	Time 1 Anx.-Amb.	Total Sample
Baldwin & Fehr, 1995 (6 samples, pooled)	12–16 weeks	80.5	57.5	32.0	67.4
Pistole, 1989	1 week	84.4	78.5	25.0	76.1
Keelan, Dion, & Dion, 1994	16 weeks	87.9	79.3	50.0	80.2
Shaver & Brennan, 1992	40 weeks	81.1	69.0	57.6	71.1
Senchak & Leonard, 1992	52 weeks	87.0	31.0	11.5	75.0
Feeney & Noller, 1992	10 weeks	81.0	73.0	53.0	75.0
Kirkpatrick & Hazan, 1994	4 years	83.0	61.0	50.0	70.0

These researchers report six studies involving mass testing of
college students, with the time lag between testing sessions varying from 12 to 16 weeks. Combined, the samples show an overall
stability rate of 67.4%; that is, just over two thirds of subjects chose
the same attachment description on each occasion. When the level
of agreement across the two occasions is adjusted for chance
(using Cohen's Kappa), the result indicates fair agreement. Note
that stability rates differ according to attachment type, as defined
by Time 1 classification; rates range from 80.5% (secure) to 32%
(anxious-ambivalent). This pattern is not unexpected, given the
high base rate for secure attachment and the low base rate for
anxious-ambivalence.

Baldwin and Fehr (1995) also report stability data supplied to
them by other researchers (Keelan, Dion, & Dion, 1994; Pistole,
1989; Senchak & Leonard, 1992; Shaver & Brennan, 1992) and

based on time intervals from 1 week to 1 year. Overall stability rates are slightly higher than for Baldwin and Fehr's samples, varying from 71% to 80%. Although Senchak and Leonard's (1992) sample is unique, involving couples undergoing the transition to marriage, it yields similar rates of stability to other samples; also, in all cases, stability is greatest for secure subjects and least for anxious-ambivalent subjects.

Finally, other researchers whose data are not included in Baldwin and Fehr's (1995) analyses report similar stability rates for the three-group measure (see Table 3.2; lower portion). Most notably, in the longest prospective study to date, Kirkpatrick and Hazan (1994) report a 4-year follow-up of a sample of newspaper respondents (Hazan & Shaver, 1990). Despite the long time interval, 70% of subjects endorsed the same attachment description on both occasions.

Scharfe and Bartholomew (1994) report the most detailed analysis of stability of the *four-group* forced-choice measure. A sample of dating, cohabiting, and married couples attended two testing sessions 8 months apart; couples completed attachment interviews and provided reports of own and partner's attachment style. All three assessment methods (interview, self-report, and partner report) yielded both a categorical measure of attachment (assignment to one of the four categories) and continuous measures of each style (discussed in the next section).

Using categorical measures, 75% of females and 80% of males showed the same attachment style on each occasion, as assessed by interviews; the corresponding figures for self-report and partner report are slightly lower. For males only, interview assessments were more stable than self-reports. The associated values of Cohen's Kappa ranged from poor to good agreement. As with the three-group measure, categories with higher base rates tend to be more stable.

In summary, these results suggest comparable stability rates for the three-group and four-group measures, although it might be expected that inclusion of the two avoidant styles would improve the reliability of classification. With either measure, approximately one in four subjects shows a change in attachment type across assessments. This figure appears to vary little with the time lag between assessments; greater stability can be expected, however, for attachment styles that are endorsed with high frequency.

Likert ratings of attachment prototypes. In terms of the three attachment prototypes, stability of Likert ratings has been assessed over intervals of 2 weeks to 8 months. Test-retest correlations generally indicate moderate stability (see Table 3.3 for a summary of these results).

Scharfe and Bartholomew (1994) assessed the stability of Likert ratings of the four attachment prototypes over an 8-month interval. Test-retest correlations for the interview method were moderate to high, and correlations for self-reports and partner-reports were somewhat lower. In contrast to findings from forced-choice measures, all attachment styles showed comparable stability.

Scharfe and Bartholomew (1994) also assessed the stability of two attachment composites, based on the four-group model of attachment (see Figure 3.1). These composites are model of self (defined by subtracting ratings of preoccupied and fearful attachment from ratings of secure and dismissing attachment) and model of other (defined by subtracting ratings of dismissing and fearful attachment from ratings of secure and preoccupied attachment). Structural equation modeling was used to assess the stability of the composites derived from interview-based ratings while controlling for the unreliability of the ratings. Results indicate high stability over time.

Multiple-item scales. Finally, stability of multiple-item attachment scales has been assessed. Collins and Read (1990) developed three scales based largely on the content of Hazan and Shaver's (1987) measure: close, depend, and anxiety. These scales were moderately stable over a 2-month interval and even over an 8-month interval. When the limited reliability of the scales is taken into account, the results suggest quite high stability (Scharfe & Bartholomew, 1994).

The two major attachment dimensions of comfort with closeness and anxiety over relationships (which overlap considerably with Collins and Read's, 1990, scales) also appear to be quite stable. Test-retest correlations for a sample of married couples over a 9-month period were moderate and were substantially

Table 3.3 Stability of Likert Ratings of the Three Attachment Prototypes

Sample	Timelag	Secure	Test-Retest Avoidant	Correlation Anx.-Amb.
Levy & Davis, 1988	2 weeks	.48	.58	.65
Feeney & Noller, 1992	10 weeks	.57	.73	.70
Hammond & Fletcher, 1991	4 months	.37	.56	.47
Shaver & Brennan, 1992	8 months	.56	.68	.56

higher when the limited reliability of the scales is taken into account (Feeney, Noller, & Callan, 1994). Similarly, the five attachment scales that have been linked to these two dimensions show acceptable stability over a 10-week interval (Feeney, Noller, & Hanrahan, 1994).

Explaining Stability and Instability

Despite the fact that there is considerable evidence for the stability of adult attachment, researchers' interpretations of this evidence varies. Scharfe and Bartholomew (1994), for example, suggest that the true stability of attachment measures is high. That is, much of the observed instability appears to stem from unreliability of measurement rather than from variability in the construct. In support of this claim, Scharfe and Bartholomew point to the finding that rates of stability do not decrease when the period of time between testing is longer; they also note the promising rates of stability obtained when the unreliability of measurement is taken into account. On the other hand, Baldwin and Fehr (1995) argue that attachment measures show considerable instability, even when the individuals studied are in stable relationships and attachment is assessed by trained interviewers.

Both of these perspectives may be valid. Certainly it appears that some of the instability in adult attachment stems from unreliability of measurement, with more refined measures showing greater stability. At the same time, there is no doubt that some instability reflects actual change in attachment patterns over time.

The latter finding is not perturbing to attachment researchers, who acknowledge that significant relationship experiences and other major life events may alter attachment patterns and associated mental models (see Chapter 1).

With regard to instability of adult attachment beyond that which stems from unreliable measures, two explanations have been advanced: The first explanation, as suggested above, is that significant life events are associated with a lack of *long-term* continuity in attachment behavior; the second explanation focuses on the possibility of *short-term* instability in individuals' attachment orientations as related to contextual factors.

Longitudinal studies have attempted to evaluate the claim that significant life events are associated with change in attachment behavior. Baldwin and Fehr (1995) report no link between stability of attachment style and a simple measure of change in relationship status. A more detailed study (Scharfe & Bartholomew, 1994) reveals scattered relations between stability of attachment and measures of life events; for example, the amount of change in interview-based attachment ratings was related to the number of positive interpersonal events. Note that in Scharfe and Bartholomew (1994), relations of this type may have been weakened by the fact that all subjects were in stable relationships.

Other studies provide stronger support for the link between stability of attachment and life events (especially relationship events). Feeney and Noller (1992) found that, for a sample of young adults, the formation of a steady relationship during the course of the study was related to change in attachment style, although there was no clear link between such relationship events and whether change was in the direction of greater security or greater insecurity. In another study of young couples, on the other hand, Hammond and Fletcher (1991) found that involvement in satisfying relationships at one point in time was associated with increased security at a later time. Kirkpatrick and Hazan's (1994) 4-year prospective study sheds further light on this issue. These researchers found that relationship experiences moderate the stability of attachment style: Relationship breakups were associated with change from secure to insecure forms of attachment, and avoidant subjects who formed new relationships were less likely to remain avoidant than those who did not.

Although there is a need for further study of the effect of relationship events on attachment patterns, it is also important to consider the alternative explanation for instability in adult attachment. According to Baldwin and Fehr (1995), there may be short-term instability in adults' state of mind with respect to attachment. That is, the individual is likely to have schemas for various types of relational expectations, developed through diverse experiences in different interpersonal contexts. His or her attachment orientation at a given point in time may reflect a subset of memories and interpersonal expectations elicited by particular situational factors operating at the time. This explanation, though tentative, is consistent with current conceptualizations of working models (as we show in Chapter 5).

Methodological Implications of Research Into Stability of Attachment

The fact that adult attachment patterns show some instability over time has implications for research procedures. In particular, it raises questions about the practice of assessing attachment style at a different point in time from other variables of interest (Baldwin & Fehr, 1995). This practice has sometimes been adopted as a matter of convenience (e.g., screening students for attachment style during mass testing sessions); at other times, it has been followed for more compelling reasons (in particular, to minimize contamination between measures of attachment style and other constructs). In any case, researchers need to bear in mind that some subjects would have described their attachment style differently at the other testing session. Note, however, that this problem can be reduced by using more reliable measures of attachment or by using multiple measures.

Similar methodological concerns prompted Kirkpatrick and Hazan (1994) to caution against simplistic interpretations of prospective studies predicting later relationship status from attachment style at an earlier time. Attachment style is more strongly related to concurrent than to later relationship status; furthermore, when later attachment style is taken into account, earlier attachment style is only weakly related to later relationship status. Hence the link between attachment style and later relationship status seems to be due primarily to the relative stability of attachment.

Longitudinal data reported by Kirkpatrick and Hazan (1994) also cast doubt on the utility of retrospective accounts of attachment style; that is, those that ask subjects to recall their attachment style at an earlier point in time. Subjects show limited ability to recall their previous attachment style; in particular, they are biased toward "recalling" their current attachment style.

*Conceptual Implications of Research Into
the Stability of Attachment: Traits Versus Relationships*

Given the available information about the extent of stability, how are adult attachment styles best conceptualized? Does the moderately high stability suggest that attachment styles are enduring, traitlike characteristics of individuals? Or do the limits to stability suggest that attachment styles reflect functioning specific to current relationships?

In their early work on adult attachment, Hazan and Shaver (1987) note that, although attachment theory emphasizes the personal characteristics associated with attachment styles, it recognizes that relationship behavior is also influenced by situational variables. A secure person trying to establish a relationship with an anxious-ambivalent partner, for example, may be pushed to act and feel avoidant. In line with this perspective, Kirkpatrick and Hazan (1994) suggest that measures of adult attachment are likely to reflect traitlike characteristics of the individual, together with relationship functioning. On the one hand, attachment styles appear to be more stable than relationships, and hence presumably tap some enduring qualities of individuals; on the other hand, it seems almost certain that responses to attachment measures are influenced by current relationship events (Kirkpatrick & Hazan, 1994).

Moreover, individual characteristics and relationship events may be bound together. By choosing particular partners, individuals are likely to find themselves in relationship situations that confirm their expectations of relationships (Collins & Read, 1990; Kirkpatrick & Davis, 1994; Kirkpatrick & Hazan, 1994).

Researchers into infant and child attachment have also discussed this possibility (see Chapter 1 in this volume). If relationship partners are chosen to confirm preexisting expectations, systematic patterns of partner matching should be evident.

Partner matching on attachment characteristics: integrating traits and relationships. Consistent with the above argument, studies of dating and married couples provide evidence of partner matching on attachment characteristics. The most robust finding is that secure individuals tend to be paired with secure partners (Collins & Read, 1990; Feeney, 1994; Senchak & Leonard, 1992). Involvement with a secure and responsive partner is likely to confirm and maintain positive working models of attachment.

There is also some evidence that avoidant individuals tend to be paired with anxious-ambivalent partners, and that the relationships of anxious-ambivalent females paired with either secure or avoidant males are relatively stable (Kirkpatrick & Davis, 1994). Again, this pattern of matching tends to confirm expectations; avoidant individuals may expect partners to be clingy and dependent, whereas anxious-ambivalent individuals may expect partners to be distant and rejecting.

Of course, findings of this kind are not easy to interpret. It is possible that secure individuals are attracted to secure partners, and hence that this "pairing" effect is evident even at the earliest stages of relationships. Alternatively, being in an ongoing relationship with a secure individual may afford the partner the opportunity to revise existing negative models of attachment figures; hence the tendency for secure individuals to be paired with secure partners may be evident only in established relationships. Resolution of such issues requires longitudinal studies that track subjects' attachment styles over the full course of relationship development.

The observed findings highlight the need for researchers working with couples to be aware of patterns of partner matching. Partner matching implies that, in studies of real relationships, subjects' attachment styles may be confounded with those of their partners. If secure individuals report high-quality relationships, this effect may stem in part from their tendency to be paired with secure partners. For this reason, researchers have been interested in the extent to which both own and partner's attachment styles are associated with relationship quality.

Effects of own and partner attachment styles. Several studies assess the implications of own and partner's attachment styles. Collins and Read (1990) found that, for dating couples, evaluations of the relationship were related to both own and partner's attachment style, as defined by the dimensions of close, depend, and anxiety. The pattern of results was largely gender specific: Men's comfort with closeness (close) was related most strongly to their own and their partner's evaluation of the relationship, whereas women's fear of abandonment (anxiety) was related most strongly to their own and their partner's evaluation of the relationship. Own and partner effects were roughly comparable in size.

Other studies of dating couples provide partial support for these results. Simpson (1990) reports reliable correlations between measures of relationship quality and both own and partner attachment styles. Consistent with Collins and Read's (1990) results, Simpson found that the most robust effect of partner attachment was the negative effect of women's anxious-ambivalence. In contrast to that study, however, effects were generally less consistent for partner attachment than for own attachment. These findings are similar to those reported by Kirkpatrick and Davis (1994) based on the three-group forced-choice measure of attachment. These researchers note that individuals' concurrent reports of dating relationships were strongly related to own attachment category: Relationships are rated more negatively by avoidant men and by avoidant and anxious-ambivalent women. The most robust effect of partner attachment was a tendency for men paired with anxious-ambivalent women to rate their relationships negatively.

Recent research addresses these issues with respect to marital relationships, using the attachment dimensions of comfort with closeness and anxiety over relationships. Feeney, Noller, and Callan (1994) found that communication patterns and marital satisfaction were related to own and partner attachment dimensions. Links were stronger for own than for partner attachment, and the relative importance of comfort and anxiety depended on gender and on the particular relationship variable being considered. In a study of relationship satisfaction across the life cycle of marriage, husbands' and wives' satisfaction was associated with levels of comfort and anxiety of both self and partner, as assessed by simple correlations (Feeney, 1994). When the independent contribution of each attachment dimension was assessed using multiple regression analysis, satisfaction was related to own anxiety (for both genders) and to own comfort (for wives only); the strongest partner effect was the negative influence of wives' anxiety on husbands' satisfaction.

In summary, there is support for the effects of both own and partner attachment on relationship quality. The most robust finding for partner attachment is the negative effect of women's anxiety on men's perceptions of their relationships. Most studies suggest that effects are stronger for own attachment than for partner attachment. This finding may be "real"; that is, perceptions of relationships may indeed be influenced more strongly by attachment style of self than by that of partner. Alternatively, the finding may be explained in methodological terms, by which the link between self-reports of attachment style and relationship quality are inflated by both measures being completed by the same respondent. The study by Feeney, Noller, and Callan (1994) suggests that the latter alternative does not explain all observed results: The greater importance of own attachment style was evident even for diary reports of relationships, completed at a different point in time and in a different setting from the attachment measures.

The studies reported above have generally investigated "partner effects" by correlating subjects' relationship evaluations with partner attachment dimensions. Other studies bearing indirectly on this issue define attachment type at the level of the couple, based on responses to categorical measures of attachment. Three couple types are typically defined: secure (in which both partners choose the secure description of the categorical measure), insecure (in which both partners choose insecure descriptions), and mixed (in which one partner chooses the secure description, and the other describes himself or herself as insecure; Feeney, 1995a; Senchak & Leonard, 1992).

A recent study of attachment and affect regulation applied this typology to dating couples' responses to relationship events involving feelings of anger, sadness, and anxiety (Feeney, 1995a). Specifically, Feeney (1995a) investigated the extent to which subjects report controlling these negative feelings by suppressing them and "bottling them up." Members of secure couples reported less suppression of negative feelings than insecure couples; in addition, they were less likely to perceive their partners as suppressing their negative feelings and as wanting them to do likewise. As might be expected, the scores of mixed couples generally fell between those of secure and insecure couples.

A study investigating marital adjustment of the three couple types yielded somewhat different results, however (Senchak & Leonard, 1992). Secure couples evidenced better marital adjustment than both mixed and insecure couples, as assessed by self-reports of marital intimacy, partner's relationship functioning, and partner's withdrawal and verbal aggression in response to conflict. The finding that mixed couples (i.e., those with one insecure spouse) show similar marital adjustment to insecure couples suggests that, in the former, the attitudes and behavior of the insecure partner may have an overriding influence on the quality of the relationship. Note, however, that because the couple is adopted as the unit of analysis in these studies, the actual role of each partner within the couple is unclear. (This typology of couples also fails to distinguish between the various forms of insecurity, such as avoidance and anxious-ambivalence; more fine-grained classification would require huge samples, if all combinations of attachment style were to be adequately represented.)

In general, then, the literature provides considerable support for the effects of both subject and partner attachment style on relationship functioning: Better relationship functioning is reported by subjects who are securely attached and by subjects whose partners are securely attached. These findings raise a further question: Do attachment styles of subjects and partners *interact* to predict relationship functioning? That is, does the effect of one partner's level of security depend on the partner's security?

Interactive effects of own and partner attachment. One of the first studies to address this issue was conducted by Pietromonaco and Carnelley (1994). Subjects were given a written profile of a hypothetical relationship partner; they were asked to imagine themselves in a relationship with that partner and to evaluate the partner and the relationship along a number of dimensions. Subjects' attachment style was assessed using Hazan and Shaver's (1987) three-group forced-choice measure, and partners' attachment style was manipulated by varying the content of the profiles to reflect secure, avoidant, or anxious-ambivalent behavior. Thus, attachment styles of self and partner were both varied; unlike studies of real couples, this procedure allows researchers to see how subjects respond to different kinds of partners.

Consistent with the results of more naturalistic studies, evaluations of the partner and the relationship were related to attachment styles of both self and partner, as indicated by a number of significant main effects. For example, ratings of negative feelings about imagined relationships showed effects of own and partner's attachment style (but no interaction between these variables). Preoccupied subjects reported more negative feelings than did secure and avoidant subjects (own attachment effect); subjects imagining a relationship with an avoidant partner reported the most negative feelings; those imagining a secure partner reported the least (partner attachment effect).

On other measures, evidence of interactions between own and partner's attachment style was obtained. For example, ratings of positive feelings about imagined relationships were influenced jointly by own and partner's attachment style. Specifically, secure subjects responded less favorably toward either type of insecure partner, whereas insecure subjects (especially avoidants) responded less favorably to an avoidant partner than to a preoccupied partner (see Figure 3.2).

By researching hypothetical relationships, Pietromonaco and Carnelley (1994) were able to manipulate partners' attachment style, allowing for the study of attachment combinations that occur infrequently in real relationships (e.g., Kirkpatrick and Davis, 1994, found no avoidant-avoidant or ambivalent-ambivalent pairs in their study of 240 dating couples). It is important to note, however, that in studies of hypothetical relationships, partner attachment characteristics are made salient by experimental procedures in a way that does not happen in real life. For this reason, it is important to see whether, in real couples, the effect of

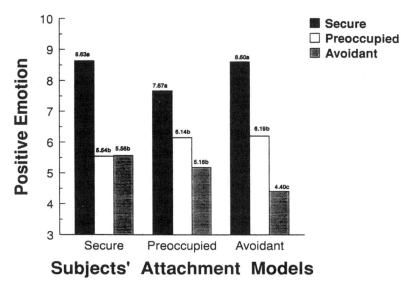

Figure 3.2. Joint Effects of Own and Partner's Attachment Styles on Positive Feelings About Relationships With Hypothetical Partners
SOURCE: Pietromonaco and Carnelley (1994).

one partner's level of security may depend on the partner's security.

This issue was explored in a recent study of married couples (Feeney, 1994). Couples sampled across the life cycle of marriage completed measures of relationship satisfaction and attachment style (defined in terms of comfort with closeness and anxiety over relationships). For the sample overall, satisfaction was related to both own and partner's attachment dimensions (main effects). Interaction effects occurred only for couples married 10 years or less; for these couples, wives' anxiety and husbands' comfort jointly affected satisfaction. Specifically, wives' anxiety was linked with dissatisfaction only for couples in which the husband was low in comfort; by contrast, husbands' anxiety was associated with low satisfaction for both partners, irrespective of wives' comfort.

These findings suggest that the anxious husband's clinging, dependent behavior may be especially destructive because it violates traditional gender-role stereotypes for men. By contrast, the anxious wife's behavior seems to confirm the female stereotype; hence it may have less harmful effects, except when she has a husband who, being uncomfortable with intimacy, does not provide the support and reassurance she craves. It is interesting to note that the pairing of a wife high in anxiety with a husband low in comfort was uncommon in longer-term marriages. This finding may explain why the interaction between wives' anxiety and husbands' comfort was restricted to more youthful marriages.

❧ Summary

In this chapter, we explore issues concerning the conceptualization and measurement of adult attachment. These issues focus not only on the psychometric properties of the various measures of attachment but also on the nature of the attachment construct. In particular, researchers have debated whether attachment measures reflect stable tendencies of the individual or current relationship functioning. These two explanations are not mutually exclusive: Both factors play a part. In the short time since research into adult attachment began, important advances in conceptualization and measurement have been made. In the next chapter, we discuss other advances that have contributed to the refining of adult attachment theory.

4

Refining the Theory
Functions and Elicitors
of Adult Attachment

The advances in attachment research outlined in Chapter 3 focus on assessment issues: What do we mean by adult attachment style? How should we measure it? What are the psychometric properties of the various measures? Complementing these advances, recent work in the area of adult attachment has focused on refining aspects of the theory itself. Based on Bowlby's (1969, 1973, 1980) theory of attachment behavior, considerable attention has been given to two interrelated issues: the functions of adult attachment behavior and the conditions under which such behavior is most likely to be elicited.

In Chapter 1, we discussed Bowlby's (1969, 1973, 1980) formulation of the functions of infant attachment behavior. These functions are proximity maintenance (establishing and maintaining contact with the attachment figure), separation protest (resisting separations from the attachment figure), secure base (using the attachment figure as a base from which to explore and master the environment), and safe haven (turning to the attachment figure for comfort and support).

Researchers have argued that these functions also apply to adult attachment behavior. Studies involving direct assessment of the four functions support this view and have helped clarify the processes involved in the development of an individual's first adult attachments. Studies linking attachment style with work and religious behaviors also highlight the secure base and safe haven functions of attachment relationships. Finally, support for the proposed functions comes from studies of attachment style differences in responses to distress (i.e., responses to threatening aspects of the physical and social environment, separations from romantic partners, and physical symptoms).

❧ The Development of Adult Attachments

Direct assessment of the four functions or components of attachment is especially relevant to the study of transition in attachments (Hazan & Zeifman, 1994). Hazan and Zeifman (1994) are interested in the processes by which young people transfer their primary attachments from parents to peers. They propose that the period between childhood and adolescence is marked by a gradual shift in the target of attachment behaviors, with some functions (components) being transferred from parents to peers earlier than others.

To test this proposition, Hazan and Zeifman (1994; Study 1) administered an interview measure of the four attachment components to a sample of children and adolescents ages 6 to 17. For each component, subjects' preferred targets were assessed by several questions; for example, "Whom do you like to spend time with?" (proximity seeking); "Whom do you miss most during separations?" (separation protest); "Whom do you feel you can always count on?" (secure base); and "Whom do you turn to for comfort when you're feeling down?" (safe haven). Because this study focused on the shift in attachments from parents to peers, targets of each function were classed simply as parents (including grandparents) or peers (friends and romantic partners).

Although all subjects in the sample preferred to spend their time in the company of peers rather than parents (proximity maintenance), other components of attachment showed clear developmental trends. A shift in the target of the safe haven function occurred between the ages of 8 and 14, with peers coming to be preferred to parents as sources of comfort and support. Only in late adolescence did peers come to replace parents with regard to separation protest and secure base functions. These results suggest that peer attachments are explored, in the first instance, from the parental base of security (Hazan & Zeifman, 1994).

In a second study, Hazan and Zeifman (1994) examined the processes by which romantic attachments develop. As in their work on early peer attachments, the focus was on the preferred targets of attachment functions. The interview measure of attachment components was administered to a sample of adults whose romantic relationships differed widely in length (some subjects were not currently in romantic relationships). Subjects were classified into three groups: not in a romantic relationship, in a relationship of less than 2 years, and in a relationship of 2 years or more. Preferred targets of attachment were also classified into three groups: parents or siblings, friends, and romantic partners.

Like the children in the earlier study, the adult sample was peer oriented in terms of proximity seeking and safe haven functions (seeking the company and support of friends or partners; see Figure 4.1). Separation protest and secure base functions were fulfilled by either parents or partners, depending on subjects' relationship status. Results suggest that the full process of attachment formation takes approximately 2 years; nearly all romantic relationships of 2 years or longer were marked by reliance on romantic partners for all four functions, compared with only one third of shorter relationships.

These findings clarify the processes by which romantic attachments develop. Just as important, they provide a framework for

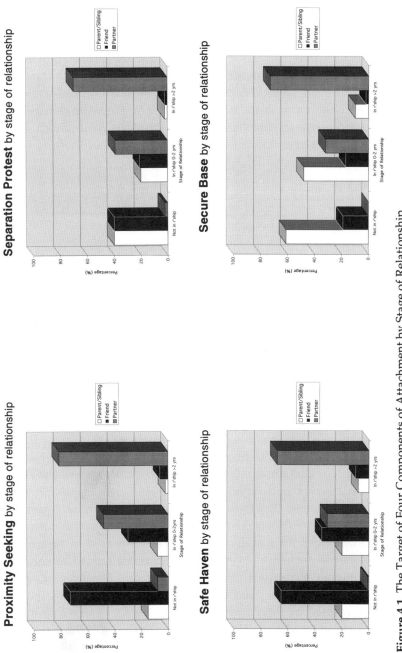

Figure 4.1. The Target of Four Components of Attachment by Stage of Relationship
SOURCE: Hazan and Zeifman (1994).

studying transition in attachments across the life span. Key questions remaining in this area include the effects of normative events, such as marriage and child rearing, on components of attachment to parents; conversely, it would be informative to assess the effect of attachments to parents on adjustment to these life events. Given societal concerns about the future care of the elderly, another important issue for researchers centers on changes in the components of attachment bonds between adult children and their parents as children come to terms with parents becoming frail and dependent (Noller & Feeney, 1994).

ᐟᐟ Love, Work, and the Secure Base

According to infant attachment theory, a key function of attachment figures is to provide a secure base from which the infant can explore the physical and social environment. Hazan and Shaver (1990) propose that, for adults, work is functionally similar to Bowlby's (1969, 1973) construct of exploration. This proposition suggests that adult attachment styles should be linked with patterns of work activity, just as infant attachment styles are linked with patterns of exploratory behavior. More specifically, just as avoidant infants appear to use exploratory behavior as a means of avoiding contact with their mothers, avoidant adults may work compulsively or use work to avoid intimate relationships. By contrast, anxious-ambivalent adults may tend to see work as an opportunity to meet unmet attachment needs; this tendency may interfere with work performance.

Hazan and Shaver (1990) tested these predictions in two questionnaire studies. Subjects completed the three-group categorical measure of attachment style, together with items that tapped orientations toward work. As expected, securely attached subjects reported higher job satisfaction than other attachment groups, thought that they were good workers, and were confident that they were valued by their coworkers. They rarely worried about work failure and did not allow work to interfere with their close relationships or their health. This relatively healthy orientation to work suggests that secure attachment provides a base from which exploration can proceed effectively.

Avoidant subjects reported similar satisfaction with job security and advancement as secure subjects. They reported greater dissatisfaction with their coworkers, however, and generally preferred to work alone. They also emphasized the importance of work success (rather than relationships), used work to avoid socializing, and reported that work interfered with their health and their relationships. This orientation to work appears to reflect a compulsive approach to activity as a way of avoiding close relationships.

Anxious-ambivalent subjects reported relatively low job satisfaction in terms of feelings of job insecurity, lack of appreciation by coworkers, and dissatisfaction with advancement. They worried about work performance and, although preferring to work with others, thought that others often intruded on their work. Anxious-ambivalent individuals also stated that they were easily distracted at work, had trouble completing projects, and tended to slacken off after praise. They reported that concerns about love relationships interfered with work and they earned a lower average income than the other attachment groups. This orientation to work reflects the preoccupation with relationships that typifies anxious-ambivalent individuals.

Thus, the three work orientations revealed in this study were largely consistent with the predictions derived from attachment theory. Hazan and Shaver (1990) recognize, however, that not all jobs provide the challenge that is implicit in the concept of exploration; for this reason, they also asked subjects to report on their leisure activities. As would be expected, avoidant subjects were the least likely to report that they spent their free time socializing and that leisure provided a renewal of social ties. Moreover, anxious-ambivalent subjects were the most likely to report that their leisure activities provided excitement and that they spent their free time shopping (an activity that lonely people may use as a way of coping with negative feelings; Rubenstein & Shaver, 1982).

Clearly, further work is needed before the associations between attachment style and patterns of work and leisure activity are fully understood. For example, we know of no published investigation that has examined these issues from the perspective of the four-group model of adult attachment. Useful information is also likely to be provided by additional work-related measures with more established psychometric properties; relevant variables here could include job involvement, job-related stress, and patterns of supervisor-peer interaction. Despite the need for further research, Hazan and Shaver's (1990) results suggest that attachment style is meaningfully related to the ways in which people balance their investments in work, leisure activities, and love relationships.

❧ Religious Behavior: God as a Secure Base and Safe Haven

As we have just seen, securely attached adults seem to maintain relatively adaptive patterns of work and leisure activity. Such a finding is consistent with the proposition that these individuals use attachment figures as a secure base, from which they can explore and master the wider physical and social environment. Similarly, theoretical and empirical work linking adult attachment styles with religious belief and behavior emphasizes attachment-related concepts such as secure base and safe haven (Kirkpatrick, 1992, 1994; Kirkpatrick & Shaver, 1992).

According to Kirkpatrick (1994), most Christians perceive themselves as having a personal relationship with God; this relationship represents the core of their religious faith. Furthermore, the relationship with God that believers experience is characterized by the defining features of attachment relationships, as outlined earlier. For example, many believers use regular prayer as a way of maintaining contact with God (proximity seeking). Belief in the existence and presence of God seems to allay fear and anxiety and to provide a sense of confidence and emotional security (secure base). Perhaps most striking, religion plays an important role for believers in times of stress, providing them with a source of comfort, support, and strength (safe haven; Kirkpatrick, 1992). In Table 4.1, we present the first lines of hymns related to each of the defining features of attachment relationships.

Table 4.1 First Lines of Hymns Related to the Defining Features of Attachment

Defining feature	First line of hymn
Proximity seeking	Abide with me, fast falls the eventide O, for a closer walk with God, a calm and heavenly frame
Secure base	Forth in Thy name, O Lord I go, my daily labor to pursue Awake my soul and with the sun, Thy daily stage of duty run
Safe haven	Rock of ages, cleft for me, let me hide myself in Thee Jesus, lover of my soul, let me to Thy bosom fly

Empirical studies applying attachment theory to the study of religious behavior have produced interesting, if somewhat complex, results. Specifically, Kirkpatrick (1992, 1994) suggests that the attachment perspective enables researchers to integrate two apparently contradictory sets of findings concerning the correlates of religious behavior.

On the one hand, empirical data provide some support for the compensation model of religious behavior, which argues that people are most likely to turn to religion during times of emotional stress and in the absence of adequate human relationships. In other words, people are inclined to compensate for their inadequate human relationships by having a close relationship with God. The compensation hypothesis is supported by studies of religious conversion: Converts typically report that their conversion experience was preceded by a period of turmoil and distress, frequently marked by serious difficulties with parental and other personal relationships. These data are consistent with the notion that the attachment system is most strongly activated under conditions of stress, and that those who fail to establish secure attachments with parents are likely to seek substitute attachment figures (Ainsworth, 1985).

On the other hand, cross-sectional data tend to support the correspondence hypothesis, which states that individual differences in relationship styles parallel differences in religious behavior.

Consistent with this hypothesis, a number of studies show that perceptions of God tend to be positively correlated with perceptions of self and the preferred parent (Kirkpatrick, 1992). Further support for the correspondence hypothesis comes from research using a simple measure of individual differences in attachment to God, modeled after Hazan and Shaver's (1987) three-group measure of general attachment style. Compared with avoidant individuals (defined in terms of general attachment style), secure individuals see God as more loving, less distant, and less controlling. Avoidant individuals show less religious commitment than those who are securely attached and are more likely than other attachment groups to be agnostic. Anxious-ambivalent individuals are the most likely to report extreme religious behaviors, such as speaking in tongues (Kirkpatrick & Shaver, 1992). These results support the proposition that mental models of attachment are relatively constant and that beliefs about attachment figures (including God) reflect prior experience with attachment relationships.

Kirkpatrick (1992) argues that these two hypotheses can be integrated by taking into account the time dimension. Hence, at any one point in time, security of (human) attachment is linked with security of attachment to God; that is, people seem to hold similar models of human and divine relationships. Insecure attachment predicts conversion experiences at a later point in time, however.

Another noteworthy finding to emerge from Kirkpatrick's work is that individual differences in security of attachment to God are strongly linked with indexes of psychological well-being and life satisfaction, although other measures of religiosity are not (Kirkpatrick & Shaver, 1992). Similarly, Noller and Clarke (1995) found that the only measure of religious belief or behavior related to mental health was a measure of attachment to God. Secure attachment to God was related to low depression, whereas believers who were fearful or preoccupied in their attachment to God were lower in self-esteem and higher in anxiety than secure or dismissing believers or nonbelievers. Given previous conflicting findings concerning the link between religiosity and well-being, these results suggest the importance of focusing specifically on security of attachment to God.

✿ Attachment Style and Responses to Distress

Attachment style has been linked with responses to environmental stressors, separations from romantic partners, and physical symptoms. The focus on responses to distress reflects theoretical work on the conditions likely to elicit attachment behavior.

Bowlby (1984) sees the attachment system in infancy as maintaining a balance between proximity seeking and exploratory behavior (see Chapter 1 of this volume). When the attachment figure is nearby and the environment is familiar, an infant shows signs of comfort and security and is likely to engage in exploratory activity. By contrast, when the infant is in a strange or threatening situation, attachment behavior is likely to be evident. Conditions that activate attachment behavior in infants are of three major types: environmental conditions, such as alarming events and rebuffs by adults or other children; conditions within the attachment relationship, such as absence, departure, or discouraging of proximity on the part of the caregiver; and conditions of the child, such as fatigue, hunger, pain, and sickness (pp. 258-259).

Although some of these specific conditions (e.g., hunger) may elicit attachment behavior only in the helpless infant, the broad typology is applicable to adult relationship behavior. Hence, by analogy, the following situations are likely to activate attachment behavior in adults: stressful social or environmental conditions, conditions seen as threatening the future of the attachment relationship (absence or discouraging of proximity on the part of the romantic partner; conflict with the partner), and conditions of the individual, such as ill health. The studies discussed below focus on behavior under these conditions. These studies support the proximity seeking, separation protest, safe haven, and secure base functions of romantic bonds and clarify the conditions under which attachment behavior is most apparent.

Responses to Environmental Stressors

Does stress elicit attachment behavior? Most of the early research into adult attachment assessed the link between attachment style and global evaluations of relationship quality. The unstated assumption behind this type of research is that attachment style influences behavior across a range of settings. This assumption is not inconsistent with attachment theory; indeed, the robust associations identified by these studies point to pervasive differences between attachment groups. Nevertheless, because attachment behavior is particularly activated under conditions of acute and chronic stress, it is precisely under these conditions that individual differences in attachment behavior should be most pronounced (Simpson et al, 1992; Simpson & Rholes, 1994).

In line with this argument, Simpson and colleagues (1992) investigated the effect of an environmental stressor on attachment behavior. Dating couples took part in a laboratory study in which the female member of each couple was told that she would shortly be "exposed to a situation and set of experimental procedures that arouse considerable anxiety and distress in most people" (p. 437). Couples were unobtrusively videotaped during the alleged "waiting" time to assess the extent to which females turned to their partners for support (support seeking) and the extent to which their partners provided support (support giving).

Attachment style was defined in terms of two self-report scales: secure versus avoidant (similar to comfort with closeness) and anxious versus nonanxious (similar to anxiety over relationships). Females' anxiety in response to the experimental situation was assessed using coders' ratings of fear and anxiety, based on the videotapes. A similar method was used to measure females' support seeking and males' support giving.

The major finding to emerge from this study (Simpson et al., 1992) is that support seeking and support giving were jointly influenced by self-reports of attachment (secure vs. avoidant) and by coders' ratings of females' anxiety. For more securely attached women, high levels of observer-rated anxiety were associated with high levels of support seeking; for more avoidant women, high levels of anxiety were associated with physical and emotional withdrawal from partners. Similarly, for more securely attached men, high levels of partner anxiety were associated with high levels of support giving; for more avoidant men, high partner anxiety was associated with low levels of support (see Figure 4.2).

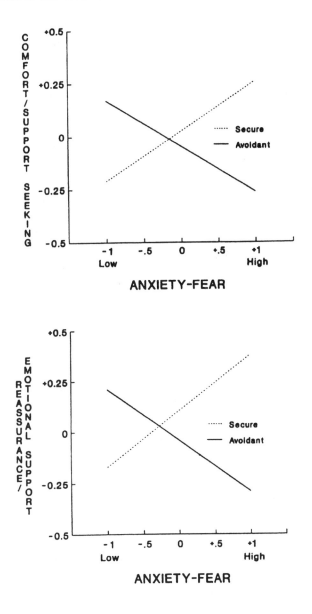

Figure 4.2. Relations Between Anxiety and Support Seeking and Support Giving for Secure and Avoidant Women and Men
SOURCE: Simpson et al. (1992).

The strong effects of attachment style observed in conditions of high anxiety were as expected, with securely attached subjects showing much more support seeking and support giving than avoidant subjects. In conditions of low anxiety, however, attachment style differences were reversed (rather than simply being weaker, as attachment theory would predict). That is, at lower levels of anxiety, avoidant individuals engaged in more support seeking and support giving than secure individuals. The reason for this result is not fully clear; Simpson et al. (1992) suggest that, under low levels of threat, avoidant persons' need for closeness may be easily aroused, having rarely been satisfied in the past.

Overall, Simpson et al.'s (1992) results highlight the importance of defining the context of interactions when describing the characteristics of a particular attachment style. It seems inappropriate, for example, to describe avoidant individuals as cold and distant (as researchers have tended to do), if such descriptors apply only to behavior under stressful conditions.

These results also suggest that, for secure individuals, overt attachment behavior (support seeking, support giving) occurs only at relatively high levels of distress. At the same time, the positive association between females' anxiety and the support given to them by secure males implies that secure persons are able to gauge, and to offer, the amount of support that partners need (Simpson & Rholes, 1994). Thus it appears that, in comparison with avoidant partners, secure partners are more effective in fulfilling the secure base and safe haven functions of attachment.

The link between attachment style and responses to environmental stress has also been studied in a more "naturalistic" setting, involving missile attacks occurring during the Gulf War (Mikulincer, Florian, & Weller, 1993). Secure, avoidant, and anxious-ambivalent attachment groups differed in their emotional reactions to the attacks: High levels of hostility and psychosomatic symptoms were reported by both avoidant and anxious-ambivalent individuals, with the latter group also reporting high levels of anxiety and depression. Furthermore, attachment groups differed in the strategies used to cope with the stressful situation: Secure individuals were more likely than the other attachment groups to seek support from others, avoidant individuals tended to distance themselves from the situation (e.g., by trying to forget about it), and anxious-ambivalent individuals focused on their emotional responses to the situation (e.g., by wishing they felt differently and by criticizing themselves). These results support the proposition that secure attachment facilitates constructive responses to stress, and highlight the contrasting features of the two major insecure groups.

Is the attachment system effective in reducing stress? The research discussed above emphasizes attachment style differences in response to environmental stressors. A complementary perspective on stress and attachment has been adopted by Kirkpatrick (Feeney & Kirkpatrick, in press; Carpenter & Kirkpatrick, 1995). Based on Bowlby's (1973) contention that the goal of the attachment system is "felt security," Kirkpatrick focuses on whether attachment figures actually serve to reduce stress in adults. Specifically, Kirkpatrick has studied the effect of the presence of attachment figures on responses to environmental stressors. Although the presence of attachment figures should reduce stress, this effect may be moderated by attachment style: Bowlby emphasizes that anxiety and fear are reduced by confidence in the availability of attachment figures, which is a feature of secure attachment.

Feeney and Kirkpatrick (in press) studied the effects of attachment security and the presence of romantic partners on females' responses to a stressful mental arithmetic task. Attachment security was defined using Simpson et al.'s (1992) two scales (secure vs. avoidant; anxious vs. nonanxious), but with scores dichotomized as high and low. Romantic partners were present for one half of the study and absent for the other; the order of these two conditions was different for different subjects.

In the first half of the study (during which some of the women had their partners present and others did not), anxious and avoidant women showed more arousal than secure women when separated from their partners, but the attachment groups did not differ in their arousal levels when partners were present. That is, secure women showed relatively low arousal regardless of whether their partners were present or not. When the partner-absent condition came first, anxious and avoidant women remained highly aroused throughout the experiment.

The apparent finding that partner proximity reduces anxiety only for insecure (anxious and avoidant) women is somewhat surprising; if the presence of attachment figures reduces stress, then secure individuals, being highly confident in their attachment figures, should derive benefit from being close to them. Feeney and Kirkpatrick (in press) suggest that, although their study was designed to explore the effects of partner proximity, it may have inadvertently caused separation anxiety in insecure subjects who were separated from their partners early in the study. Hence, the results may reflect insecure subjects' anxiety concerning separation and reunion.

In a follow-up study, Carpenter and Kirkpatrick (1995) tried to minimize separation anxiety by having subjects complete the partner-present and partner-absent conditions on different occasions. Female members of dating couples were led to anticipate an unknown stressful situation (Simpson et al., 1992). Anxious and avoidant women showed more arousal when partners were present than when they were absent; by contrast, results for secure women showed no effects of partner proximity. This study is important in suggesting that partner proximity may actually exacerbate stress for insecure subjects. Secure women's apparent failure to benefit from the presence of attachment figures, however, is again somewhat surprising. Perhaps secure individuals function equally well in stressful situations whether the partner is present or not, given their confidence that the partner is generally available to provide support. Clearly, more research is needed to clarify the conditions under which attachment figures serve as a source of comfort and security.

Responses to Conditions Threatening the Attachment Relationship

As we noted earlier, a number of conditions may be seen as threatening the future of an attachment relationship between two adults. These include absence or discouraging of proximity on the part of the romantic partner, and conflict with the partner. Researchers have recently begun to study how the different attachment styles respond to these conditions.

In a review article, Vormbrock (1993) argues that attachment theory can be usefully applied to research on marital separations and reunions. She reviewed the literature on spouses' responses to wartime separations and to short-term and long-term job-related separations. Although these types of separation differ in important ways (duration, frequency, predictability, etc.), spouses' reactions to the different types of separation are very similar. This finding suggests that a single theoretical framework is adequate to explain responses to marital separations. Moreover, observed stages in responses to marital separations (protest, despair, detachment) are similar to those seen in children who are separated from their caregivers; this similarity supports the relevance of attachment theory to marital bonds.

Vormbrock's (1993) analysis of marital separations focuses on universal patterns of response rather than on individual differences related to attachment style. In fact, few studies to date have examined attachment style differences in adults' responses to separations from attachment figures. The studies we discuss next have explored this issue in relation both to wartime separation and to more routine instances of separation.

Like Mikulincer et al. (1993), Cafferty and his colleagues studied behavior related to the Gulf War (Cafferty, Davis, Medway, O'Hearn, & Chappell, 1994). Rather than focusing on the wartime environment, however, Cafferty et al. studied reunion dynamics among couples in which the male spouse was deployed overseas during the war. Four months after reunion, the men and their wives completed self-report questionnaires assessing attachment style, relationship satisfaction, conflict, and affect during reunion.

For both deployed men and their wives, secure attachment was associated with higher marital satisfaction and with less postreunion conflict. Preoccupied subjects showed particularly low levels of satisfaction and particularly high levels of conflict. Links between attachment style and affect during reunion were confined to men, for whom secure attachment was associated with reports of more positive and less negative affect. The stronger results for affect among the deployed men may reflect the more stressful and less familiar nature of their separation experience.

A recent study of dating couples relates attachment style to responses to separation from partners and to situations involving attachment figures' discouraging of proximity (Feeney, 1995b). Recall that any event that is seen as threatening the future of an attachment relationship should be experienced as stressful. Hence it is important to study not only physical separation but also conditions in which there is conflict between partners, particularly over attachment-related issues such as distance and closeness.

The study reported by Feeney (1995b) involved two parts. In the first part, members of the dating couples independently provided open-ended reports of their experiences of being physically separated from the partner at some point in the relationship. Content analyses indicated that secure attachment was associated with less insecurity in response to separation, more constructive (problem-focused) coping strategies, and the perception that the separation experience strengthened the relationship.

The second part of the study involved couples' participation in three conflict-centered interactions. One of these interactions involved conflict over a specific issue (couples' use of leisure time); the remaining two were designed to elicit attachment-related anxiety by having one partner rebuff the other's attempts to maintain closeness (the role of the distant, discouraging partner was adopted by the male in one interaction and by the female in the other). At the beginning of this part of the study, subjects ("insiders") rated their expectations of their partners' behavior and motives; after each interaction, they also rated their own discomfort, and their own satisfaction with the interaction. Based on videotapes of the interactions, independent coders ("outsiders") rated subjects' affect, nonverbal behaviors, and conversation patterns.

In terms of insider ratings, secure attachment was related to positive expectations of partners' behavior and motives and to less discomfort and greater satisfaction with both issue-based and relationship-based conflict. Secure attachment was also linked with outsider ratings of less negative affect, less avoidant nonverbal behavior, and more constructive conversation patterns in response to partners' distancing behavior; by contrast, attachment was unrelated to outsider ratings of responses to the issue-based (leisure time) conflict. These results neatly integrate two separate findings reported by previous researchers: attachment style exerts very pervasive effects on *global perceptions* of relationship functioning; at the same time, attachment style differences in *observable behavior* are strong only under conditions that seem to threaten the individual or the attachment relationship.

Health Behaviors

In our discussion of attachment style and responses to distress, the emphasis so far has been on the behavior of partners in romantic relationships. By contrast, in this section we focus on individuals' reports of health behaviors. This work is important for three interrelated reasons. First, Bowlby (1969) argues that certain conditions of the individual, such as ill health, are likely to activate the attachment system; hence attachment groups should differ in their responses to unusual or distressing physical symptoms. Second, as we explain in more detail shortly, this work is consistent with theory linking attachment style with affect regulation (see Chapters 1 and 2). Finally, this work raises issues concerning attachment and support seeking, similar to those explored by Simpson et al. (1992) in the context of couple behavior.

There are compelling reasons for expecting attachment style to have implications for health. First, much empirical literature points to the health implications of various aspects of personal relationships. The more traditional research in this area has established links between health outcomes and variables such as social insecurity and social support (Cohen, 1988; Vaux, 1988). In addition, exciting new research has related the quality of specific personal relationships to physiological indexes of health. Laboratory studies have shown, for example, that hostile responses to marital conflict are associated with deterioration in functioning of the immune system, a finding that suggests important long-term implications for health (e.g., Kiecolt-Glaser et al., 1993).

The research outlined above focuses mainly on the links between relationship variables and *health status*. Links between attachment style and *health behaviors* are also to be expected.

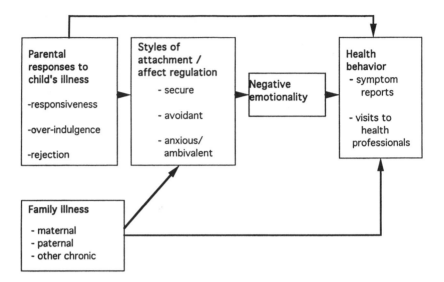

Figure 4.3. Theoretical Model Linking Family and Attachment Variables to Health Behavior
SOURCE: Feeney (1994).

Attachment theory has been called a theory of affect regulation. That is, individual differences in attachment styles reflect rules and strategies that children learn about handling negative emotion. Although these rules are learned through experiences of caregivers' responses to attachment-related distress, they are generalized to other distressing situations. Hence, attachment style should be related to responses to pain and illness.

Feeney and Ryan (1994) propose a comprehensive model linking attachment style and health variables (see Figure 4.3). This model includes three key components: early family experiences of illness, attachment style, and adult health behaviors. According to the model, early family experiences of illness (frequent or serious illness in members of the immediate family, and parental responses to the child's physical complaints) are likely to exert a direct influence on adult health behaviors, as suggested by previous research, driven primarily by social learning theory. Early family experiences of illness may also influence the development of attachment style by affecting the availability and quality of parenting.

Attachment style, in turn, is likely to have implications for health behaviors. Anxious-ambivalent persons, for example, are thought to show heightened awareness of distress; for this reason, they may be prone to reporting many symptoms. Note here the remaining component of the model, however. Negative emotionality (a general dimension of subjective distress) is included because of evidence that this variable affects responses to measures of both health and stress-personality (Watson & Pennebaker, 1989). Hence it is possible that any tendency for anxious-ambivalent subjects to report physical symptoms may be explained, in part, by their general tendency to perceive events negatively.

The model proposed by Feeney and Ryan (1994) was assessed in a short-term longitudinal study, in which a large sample of undergraduate students completed self-report questionnaires. The main focus of the research was on measures of early family illness, attachment style, and negative emotionality, assessed at the start of the study, as predictors of health behaviors occurring during the following 10 weeks. Two major health behaviors were assessed: symptom-reporting and visits to health professionals.

As expected, early family experiences of illness were linked with adult health behaviors; for example, subjects reporting chronic illness in the immediate family during their childhood paid more visits to health professionals than other subjects. Early family experiences of illness were also linked with attachment style. Reports that parents had been overindulgent when the child complained of ill-health were related positively to anxious-ambivalent attachment and negatively to avoidant attachment; in addition, reports that parents often cut back on their normal activities because of ill health were related to insecure forms of attachment.

In terms of the implications of attachment style for adult health behaviors, two key findings emerged. First, as expected, anxious-ambivalent attachment was linked with symptom reporting, but this link was weakened when the influence of negative emotionality was taken into account. Second, avoidant attachment was inversely related to visits to health professionals. Even when the level of physical symptoms was controlled, this association remained reliable.

Feeney and Ryan's (1994) findings support the link between attachment style and health behaviors. They also highlight the need to consider attachment as a multidimensional construct rather than simply in terms of security-insecurity. That is, anxious-ambivalent and avoidant attachment represent fundamentally different ways of responding to attachment figures and to distressing situations. The relatively high level of symptom reporting among anxious-ambivalent subjects supports the notion that these subjects focus on signs of distress. By contrast, the relatively low levels of medical help seeking among avoidant subjects are consistent with their general tendency to avoid seeking support and advice; in the medical context, there are clearly important implications of such delayed help seeking.

❧ Summary

The studies discussed in this chapter support the proposition that the functions of attachment behavior in adults are analogous to those in infants: proximity seeking, separation protest, secure base, and safe haven. These studies also provide evidence that differences between attachment groups, although evident in a range of settings, are most pronounced under stressful conditions. In attempting to establish the universal functions of attachment behavior, researchers have shown that attachment theory can clarify phenomena as diverse as workplace behaviors and religious attitudes. Much further work remains to be done in this area, however, before we can claim to understand how the common functions of attachment behavior are manifested by particular attachment styles.

5

❧

Attachment Style,
Working Models,
and Communication

❧ Working Models of Attachment

As we discuss in Chapter 1, the concept of inner working models is central to Bowlby's (1969) theory of attachment. These inner working models (or mental representations) are proposed by Bowlby as the mechanism by which early attachment experiences affect a person throughout life. Bowlby postulates that, to be able to predict and manage their world, individuals need both a model of their environment (environmental model) and a model of their own skills and potentialities (organismic model). Bowlby sees these inner working models as analogous to maps and plans, being

91

used to simulate and predict the behavior of others in social interaction, as well as to plan one's own behavior to achieve relational goals.

Inner working models are thought to develop out of the child's relationship history, as the child explores his or her relationships through such behaviors as demands for attention and comfort. When parents are supportive and cooperative in their interactions with their children, the children are likely to develop inner working models that enable them to have positive relationships with others, as well as to explore the environment with a sense of confidence and mastery.

Although working models are initially very simple, they become more sophisticated with development. As Bowlby (1969) explains,

> In human beings, psychological development is characterized not only by simple systems' being superseded by goal-corrected systems, but also by the individual's becoming increasingly aware of the set-goals he has adopted, by his developing increasingly sophisticated plans for achieving them, and by his increasing ability to relate one plan to another, to detect incompatibility between plans and to order them in terms of priority. (pp. 153-154)

Adults' models of attachment are likely to reflect the complexity and density (more interconnections) of the networks of relationships typical of adults.

As Bretherton (1985) points out, inner working models enable new situations to be faced with the benefit of previous experience. The working models formed early in life are assumed to remain influential throughout life, although they tend to be adjusted in response to new experiences. Bretherton also argues that revision of working models is crucial, particularly in childhood, when development is fairly rapid and change is the norm. Bowlby (1969) maintains, however, that changes to working models are generally minor in scope. Major changes in either the person or the environment may lead to more dramatic revisions of working models, although Bowlby sees change as slow and difficult, even in these circumstances.

Later in this chapter, we examine factors affecting the stability of working models. At this point, it is important to realize that Bowlby (1969) does not claim that working models are stable throughout life, although he does claim that early experience with the primary caregiver is very influential in the models developed in childhood. Children with responsive caretakers tend to develop models of the self as worthy of care and of others as trustworthy (Bretherton, 1985; Sroufe & Waters, 1977). Given a consistent pattern of caregiving, these working models are expected to become solidified through repeated experience (Collins & Read, 1994).

The importance that Bowlby (1973) places on childhood experiences can be seen in the following quotation:

> When information about a child's experiences of interaction with parents and parent figures is obtained—usually partly from first-hand observation of family members who are interviewed together and partly from the family's history as it is pieced together, often only slowly and from a diversity of sources—the forecasts the child makes of how attachment figures are likely to behave towards him are not unreasonable extrapolations from his experiences of the way in which they have behaved towards him in the past, and may perhaps still be behaving towards him in the present. (pp. 207-208)

In other words, inner working models are seen by Bowlby (1973) as developing in a fairly stable family setting and as reflecting the social reality (positive or negative) experienced by the individual. Main et al. (1985) also argue that these inner working models are generalized beliefs and expectations, based on a child's attempts to gain comfort and security, and success or otherwise at doing so.

Given that working models center around the regulation and fulfillment of attachment needs, they are most likely to be activated automatically when attachment-relevant events (e.g., those that create stress) occur (Collins & Read, 1994; Simpson et al., 1992). In such situations, working models operate largely outside of conscious awareness. How easily a working model is accessed depends on the amount of experience on which it is based and how often the individual has applied the model and found it to work (Collins & Read, 1994). Bowlby (1969) suggests that much psychopathology can be regarded as the consequence of "models that are in greater or lesser degree inadequate or inaccurate. . .because [they are] totally out-of-date, or because [they are] only half revised. . .or because [they are] full of inconsistencies or confusions" (p. 82).

One reason that working models are likely to be resistant to change is that they are frequently self-fulfilling (Collins & Read, 1994). Actions based on these models produce consequences that reinforce them. For example, individuals who believe that others do not care about them may approach a whole range of situations defensively; as a consequence, they may be less likely to get their needs met and more likely to have their negative models of self and other reinforced. Watzlawick (1983) relates a story in which a man considers asking his neighbor if he can borrow a hammer. Unfortunately, the scenario he plays out in his head for this potential interaction leads him not to make a reasonable request of his neighbor, but rather to knock on his neighbor's door and tell him that he can keep his d----- hammer. Thus, this man's negative model of other is reinforced not by the neighbor's behavior, but by his own inner working model of the neighbor and the neighbor's likely response.

Collins and Read (1994) take the view that it is unreasonable to assume that working models reflect the quality of parent-child relationships alone. Relationships with other attachment figures such as siblings and grandparents may also be influential. In addition, as children get older, relationships with peers are likely to have an effect. For example, if children become the victims of bullying, those experiences will have an effect on their models of other and perhaps even on their models of self, because they have to cope with the possibility that they are the kind of person whom others dislike and even want to hurt.

Bowlby (1973) claims that the insecure child may have mutually inconsistent working models of the same attachment figure, particularly in families where the child's actual experiences in interaction with the parent differ markedly from what the parent tells the child. In one model, which is highly accessible to awareness, the child sees the parent as primarily good and takes the blame for the parent's bad or rejecting behavior. In the second model, which is defensively excluded from awareness, the child experiences resentment against the parent. Bretherton (1985) notes that this defensive exclusion of threatening information interferes with the updating of working models; the idealized model does not correspond to reality and is unlikely to be corrected when significant changes in the environment occur.

As noted in Chapter 1, there is also some evidence that individuals may develop different models in different relationships. For example, an individual may be secure with mother but insecure with father. Collins and Read (1994) suggest that individuals develop a hierarchy of working models, with a set of generalized models at the top of the hierarchy, models for particular classes of relationships (e.g., family members, peers) at an intermediate level, and models for particular relationships (e.g., father, spouse) at the lowest level (see Figure 5.1). As a general principle, models high in an individual's hierarchy apply to a wide range of others but tend to be less predictive for any specific situation or relationship. On the other hand, models lower in the hierarchy are highly predictive for particular relationships but less predictive for relationships in general.

According to Bretherton (1985), models of self and models of other cannot be understood without reference to each other. For example, a child who experiences the attachment figure as behaving in rejecting ways is likely to develop a negative model of both self and other. Bretherton claims that individuals internalize both sides of a relationship (e.g., the mother and the child) and are able to use both as models for their own behavior. Several studies show that parents' internal models of childhood attachment (i.e., the ones they internalized as children) govern the ways in which they behave as attachment figures to their own children (Main & Goldwyn, 1985; Ricks & Noyes, 1984).

Individual differences in attachment style reflect systematic differences in these underlying models of self and others, as formed in early childhood and modified through subsequent experience. As Main et al. (1985) note, the three attachment styles identified by Ainsworth and her colleagues (Ainsworth et al., 1978) are best thought of as "terms referring to particular types of internal work-

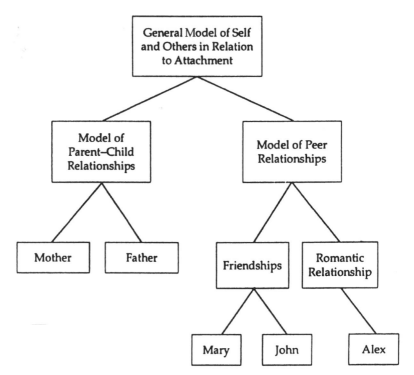

Figure 5.1. Hierarchical Structure of Working Models
SOURCE: Collins and Read (1994).

ing models of relationships, models that direct not only feelings and behavior but also attention, memory and cognition" (p.67). Consequently, Collins and Read (1994) suggest that working models should be thought of as including four interrelated components:

1. Memories of attachment-related experiences (particularly those involving the primary attachment figure)
2. Beliefs, attitudes, and expectations of self and others in relation to attachment

3. Attachment-related goals and needs
4. Strategies and plans for achieving attachment-related goals

These authors argue that these four components of working models are likely to vary across attachment groups, as detailed below. A summary of the differences in these components, using the three-group attachment model proposed by Hazan and Shaver (1987), is presented in Table 5.1.

Memories of Attachment-Related Experiences

Early studies of adult attachment, involving retrospective reports of relationships with parents, show that secure individuals tend to remember their parents as warm and affectionate, avoidant individuals remember their mothers as cold and rejecting, and anxious-ambivalent individuals remember their fathers as unfair (Collins & Read, 1990; Feeney & Noller, 1990; Hazan & Shaver, 1987; Rothbard & Shaver, 1994). These findings are in line with predictions from attachment theory. One problem with retrospective reports, of course, is that we cannot be sure to what extent memories are affected by current views of the world and overall satisfaction with life. Research on the effects of mood on memories of childhood suggests that the individual's current state does have an effect on such memories, although Parker (1983) shows that these effects are not strong.

Attachment-Related Beliefs and Attitudes

The beliefs and attitudes of secure subjects are consistent with their higher self-esteem and self-confidence (Feeney & Noller, 1990; Feeney, Noller, & Hanrahan, 1994). They have few self-doubts and a high sense of self-worth. They tend to be interpersonally oriented and to see themselves as generally liked by others. In addition, they see others as well-intentioned and good hearted, as well as dependable, trustworthy, and altruistic. In other words, the beliefs and attitudes of secure individuals reflect their positive models of both self and others.

Table 5.1 Attachment Group Differences in Working Models

Secure	Avoidant	Anxious-Ambivalent
Memories		
Parents warm and affectionate	Mothers cold and rejecting	Fathers unfair
Attachment-Related Beliefs, Attitudes		
Few self doubts; high in self-worth	Suspicious of human motives	Others complex and difficult to understand
Generally liked by others	Others not trustworthy or dependable	People have little control over own lives
Others generally well-intentioned and good-hearted	Doubt honesty and integrity of parents and others	
Others generally trustworthy, dependable, and altruistic	Lack confidence in social situations	
Interpersonally oriented	Not interpersonally oriented	
Attachment-Related Goals and Needs		
Desire intimate relationships	Need to maintain distance	Desire extreme intimacy
Seek balance of closeness and autonomy in relationships	Limit intimacy to satisfy needs for autonomy and independence	Seek lower levels of autonomy
	Place greater weight on goals such as achievement	Fear rejection
Plans and Strategies		
Acknowledge distress	Manage distress by cutting off anger	Heightened displays of distress and anger to get response
Modulate negative affect in constructive way	Minimize distress-related emotional displays; withhold intimate disclosure	Solicitous and compliant to gain acceptance

The beliefs and attitudes of avoidant individuals contrast with those of secure individuals, particularly in terms of beliefs about others. Avoidant individuals tend not to be interpersonally oriented; rather, because of their lack of confidence in social situations, they may be minimally involved in social relationships. They tend to see others as not trustworthy or dependable, to doubt their honesty and integrity, and to be suspicious of their motives.

Anxious-ambivalent individuals see others as complex and difficult to understand. For this reason, they are wary (or perhaps ambivalent) about interacting with them. They also see themselves (and people in general) as having little control over their own lives.

Attachment-Related Goals and Needs

Secure individuals desire intimate relationships but prefer a balance between closeness and autonomy in relationships. That is, they are comfortable with closeness but they also value autonomy and are happier in relationships where needs for both closeness and autonomy can be met.

For avoidant persons, important goals are maintaining distance and preventing others from getting too close. Their tendency to limit intimacy may be motivated by a strong need to avoid rejection; alternatively, this behavior may be motivated by concerns for autonomy, as reflected in an emphasis on achievement. As we showed in the earlier section on attachment and work, avoidant individuals are likely to emphasize achievement and work to avoid intimacy.

Anxious-ambivalent individuals, like those who are secure, desire intimate relationships, although these relationships are often stressful for them. These individuals tend to fear rejection and abandonment and spend a lot of time preoccupied in thinking about (mostly worrying about) their relationships. Despite the stress associated with close relationships, anxious-ambivalent individuals seek extreme intimacy and are willing to forgo autonomy needs to have their needs for intimacy met.

Plans and Strategies

As we noted when discussing affect regulation, secure individuals tend to acknowledge their distress and to deal with their negative affect in constructive ways. They are not likely to bottle up their anger and distress or to express these emotions in destructive ways (throwing tantrums, attacking others, etc.). Instead, they express these emotions in ways appropriate to the level of distress. In addition, they are able to seek help from others when they need to.

Avoidant individuals tend to minimize or even deny their emotional reactions and are less likely than others to express their emotions or let others know about their distress. As a result, they have difficulty seeking help from others to deal with their negative emotions. These individuals even have trouble seeking help from professionals such as doctors.

Anxious-ambivalent individuals are very aware of their emotional reactions and, because of their low levels of self-esteem and their heightened levels of anxiety, they tend to experience more distress than others. They are also likely to engage in heightened displays of distress to get a response from the partner or other interactant. On the other hand, in line with their high need for others' approval (Feeney, Noller, & Hanrahan, 1994), they are also inclined to be overly solicitous and compliant and to deny their own needs for fear of being rejected.

Summary

When one considers the various components of working models, it becomes clear that the memories, beliefs, goals, and strategies of secure individuals are consistent with their high levels of trust and self-esteem. Their memories of attachment figures are largely positive, as are their attitudes to others, and they enjoy being involved in close relationships. In addition, they are prepared to express their emotions in constructive ways and to seek support from others when necessary.

The memories, beliefs, goals, and strategies of avoidant individuals are consistent with their concerns about others getting too close. They are inclined to be negative about close relationships in general and particularly about intimate disclosures. They tend to be suspicious and wary of others and their motives, and to keep their emotional reactions to themselves.

The memories, beliefs, goals, and strategies of anxious-ambivalent individuals are also in line with their low self-esteem and preoccupation with relationships. Because they have difficulty coping by themselves, they are likely to be clingy and dependent. Through their demandingness and intense emotional displays, however, they may bring about the very outcomes they fear most.

❧ Functions of Working Models

How do working models function to affect our relationships with others? Collins and Read (1994) claim that these models shape our cognitive, emotional, and behavioral responses to others. Internal working models are seen as affecting how data are selected and interpreted, how we evaluate others and our relationships with them, and the plans we conceive for dealing with our relationships with other people. We will look at each of these response patterns separately to understand the various effects of working models.

Cognitive Response Patterns

One way that working models affect cognitive responses is through selective attention. In other words, our working models direct us to pay attention to certain aspects of the stimuli that confront us and to ignore other aspects. Collins and Read (1994) suggest that individuals are likely to be particularly sensitive to goal-related stimuli and to notice information that is consistent with their existing beliefs and attitudes and that is easily assimilated to existing knowledge structures. What individuals select depends on the accessibility of particular constructs contained in their working models. Given that anxious-ambivalent adults are motivated to seek approval and avoid rejection, they are likely to

be particularly sensitive to any suggestions of criticism or rejection and to overreact to these. Avoidant adults, on the other hand,
because of their concerns about others getting too close and their
suspicions about others' trustworthiness, may be particularly sensitive to signs of intrusion and control.

A second way that working models affect cognitive responses is
by creating biases in memory encoding and retrieval. Collins and
Read (1994) suggest that strong, well-established schema (such as
working models) bias memory retrieval in such a way that
schema-relevant and schema-consistent information is most likely
to be remembered. Retrieval processes are not the only ones affected; individuals may also recall or reconstruct features that
never took place, particularly as memories of actual incidents
fade. Thus someone who is particularly negative in terms of model
of other and who is sensitive to attempts at control may recreate
past situations that are only partly remembered (e.g., recalling
incidents of control that did not really happen or recalling an
occasional incident as occurring more frequently than it actually
did). Evidence suggests that recalled memories generally confirm
existing models of self and other, whether these are positive or
negative. In addition, those with a negative attachment history
(e.g., involving loss of loved ones or abuse by them) tend to have
a more elaborate knowledge of those painful experiences than of
any pleasant experiences.

A third way that working models affect cognitive responses is
through their effect on inference and explanation processes. There
is evidence that working models affect the ways individuals make
sense of their relationships. For example, Sarason and colleagues
(Pierce, Sarason & Sarason, 1992) carried out a study in which all
the children in a group received the exact same note, purported to
be from their mothers. Although the notes were identical, the
children interpreted the notes in different ways, in line with their
beliefs about the supportiveness of their mothers. Those who
perceived their mothers as generally unavailable to them saw the
notes as much less supportive than those who had more positive
beliefs about the availability of their mothers.

Collins (in press) reports a study in which subjects were asked
to provide, with respect to a hypothetical relationship, open-

ended explanations for six partner behaviors that were potentially negative. Four of these behaviors were designed to activate attachment themes and included "left you standing alone at a party" and "didn't respond when you tried to cuddle." Explanations by secure subjects reflected stronger perceptions of love and security and greater confidence in the partner's responsiveness than did those of other subjects. The explanations of preoccupied subjects reflected perceptions of others as unresponsive and rejecting. Avoidant subjects also provided negative explanations, but, in line with what we showed in Chapter 2 about their tendency to play down their emotional reactions, they denied that they would experience any emotional distress in response.

Emotional Response Patterns

In line with Bradbury and Fincham's (1987) model of affect and cognition in marriage, Collins and Read (1994) discuss the effects of working models on emotional response patterns in terms of primary and secondary appraisals. Primary appraisal involves a direct path from the working model to the emotional response, evoking the immediate emotional reaction to a particular situation. Two main mechanisms are seen as driving the primary appraisal: schema-triggered affect and goal structures. Thus, an individual who is particularly sensitive to messages of rejection and whose goal is closeness and intimacy is likely to react with great distress to such stimuli as a partner being late, failing to telephone, or forgetting a special occasion.

The emotional response that is the outcome of the primary appraisal may also affect later cognitive processing. Strong affect influences selective attention, and strong negative affect such as anger or depression may lead to a negatively biased search process; those who are depressed, for example, tend to focus on data that support their negative mood. Thus, an individual with a perennially negative model of self may focus on instances of failure and ignore experiences of success. This selective focus on negative experiences is strengthened by the fact that mood-congruent events are more salient (Bower & Cohen, 1982).

As noted earlier, emotions may also affect memory, given that individuals tend to remember material consistent with their current mood. Thus, the depressed individual described above will recall negative instances from the past and ignore any positive events that might have occurred. Similarly, a person who is particularly sensitive to attempts at control will tend, when feeling low, to recall instances consistent with that concern. In other words, affect that stems from the activation of negative working models may restrict an individual's cognitive and attention resources; as a consequence, he or she will tend to rely on overlearned schema and to react in less constructive ways.

Secondary appraisal involves the path from cognitive processing to emotional responses; in other words, how does the individual feel once he or she has taken into account his or her cognitive reaction, for example, via self-talk (Burns, 1980)? Cognitive processing may affect the initial emotional response in at least three ways: The initial response can be maintained, amplified, or lessened, depending on how the individual interprets the experience. For example, someone who was initially elated at being asked out on a date might maintain that elation by focusing on the potential fun of the date, might amplify that elation by imagining a rosy future with the dating partner, or might lessen that elation by assuming that the partner will never ask for another date.

Individuals respond to others' behavior in terms of the symbolic meaning of that behavior for themselves and for their relationship. Those who interpret the partner's failure to call when he or she was running late as indicating a lack of caring are likely to react with anger and distress (Collins, in press). On the other hand, those who interpret failure to call as related to the partner's "busyness" and level of stress may feel sorry for the partner rather than angry. How the situation is interpreted depends on the history of that behavior in the relationship, as well as more general working models of the person doing the interpreting.

Behavioral Response Patterns

As we have already noted, there is now quite a lot of evidence that those with different attachment styles behave differently in relationships. The point we are making here, however, is that those with different attachment styles behave differently because they think and feel differently (Collins & Read, 1994).

According to Collins and Read (1994), there are two mechanisms by which internal working models affect behavior. The first is through the plans and strategies stored as part of working models; the second is through working models affecting new plans being made in the current situation. An example of a stored strategy might be an individual "running home to mother" every time he or she has an argument with the spouse. Such behavior is likely to have developed as a strategy in childhood and to have carried on through adolescence and adulthood. In the current situation, working models may affect decisions such as whether to discuss the problem openly with the partner or whether to avoid the issue.

In planning behavior, secure adults tend to integrate cognitive and emotional considerations and not to be dominated by either one. Anxious-ambivalent adults focus on emotional rather than on cognitive factors. An example of this pattern is a person whose anxiety about gaining the approval of others stops him or her from attending a function he or she knows is important for career advancement. In contrast, avoidant adults overrely on cognitive factors and ignore or deny emotional reactions such as anxiety and fear. For example, an avoidant individual may see attendance at parties or other social activities as a waste of time, but may be unaware of anxiety about meeting with others.

⮆ Stability and Change in Working Models

Bowlby (1969, 1973) emphasizes that working models are active constructions that can be modified in response to experience. In line with Bowlby's theorizing, more generalized schemas are likely to remain largely intact, but individuals may construct subtypes that elaborate their existing schema (Collins & Read, 1994). So, for example, not all others may be seen as untrustworthy, just particular others.

The stability of working models may be affected by the tendency of old models to be activated more readily, particularly in times of stress. Before new constructive behaviors are activated under stress, these responses must be thoroughly learned and practiced. In addition, significant changes need to occur in the patterns of feeling and thinking that have cued the destructive behavior in the past. This kind of change requires direct attention to patterns of feeling and thinking and a determination to reject and replace maladaptive patterns actively (Devine, 1989). In the next two sections, we consider both factors that promote stability in working models and factors that promote change.

Conditions Promoting Stability

A number of factors promote the stability of working models. Perhaps the most pervasive factor is the tendency for individuals to select environments consistent with their beliefs about self and other. Such selection applies to choices such as careers and jobs, but also to the choice of a romantic partner or spouse. For example, as we showed earlier, there is evidence that relationships involving an avoidant male and anxious-ambivalent female are quite stable (although not necessarily happy); the avoidant male fulfills the anxious-ambivalent female's expectations that partners are not as concerned about love relationships as she is, and the clingy, dependent anxious-ambivalent female confirms the avoidant male's belief that it is unwise to let others get too close. What may make this partnership particularly potent is that sex role stereotypes are also being confirmed.

A second factor promoting stability in working models is the self-perpetuating nature of these models, creating the kind of information processing biases discussed earlier. When a particular model is activated, it affects what is noticed, what is remembered, and how events are explained. Thus, a person who believes that others cannot be trusted may take particular note of information supporting that conclusion, remember instances when his or her trust was betrayed, and explain current problems with the partner in terms of lack of trust.

A third factor promoting the stability of working models is the tendency for particular kinds of behavior to occur automatically, once a particular attachment model is activated. These automatic responses occur in much the same way that the small child rushes back to the safety of the attachment figure when a large dog appears on the scene.

A fourth factor relevant to the stability of working models is the tendency for these models to be self-fulfilling, by increasing the likelihood that a person with a particular model will elicit the response from others that he or she fears most. For example, the clingy and possessive behavior of the anxious-ambivalent individual is likely to drive romantic partners away and bring about a sense of abandonment.

Conditions Promoting Change

Just as some factors promote the stability of working models, others lead to change. Working models are most likely to change around major life transitions such as leaving home, getting married, having a baby, or experiencing divorce or death of a loved one. These events represent significant changes in a person's social environment that may disconfirm existing models (Collins & Read, 1994). For example, becoming involved in a stable, satisfying relationship may lead to change for those whose models of self and other have led to skepticism about the possibility of having such a relationship. The high percentage of secure subjects generally found in samples of stable couples confirms this effect (Feeney, Noller, & Callan, 1994; Senchak & Leonard, 1992).

Similarly, a secure person who is involved in a particularly negative relationship may become insecure as a result of that experience. Of course, the effect of such experiences is likely to depend on how long they last and the extent to which they are seen as emotionally significant. In their sample of young romantic partners, Hammond and Fletcher (1991) found that relationship events predicted later attachment style, as well as attachment style predicting later relationship events.

Working models may also change as individuals arrive at new understandings or new interpretations of their past experiences, particularly those that are attachment related. For example, therapeutic intervention might help individuals come to a new understanding about the breakup of their parents' marriages; in this way, they may be able to deal with their sense of betrayal and feel more positive about themselves and others. Over time (and with some positive relationship experiences), they may come to trust people again. In other words, real positive change is most likely to come about through the combination of new insights and more positive relationship experiences.

❧ Attachment and Parent-Child Communication

Bowlby (1969, 1973) links working models of attachment and communication when he suggests that internal working models of self and caregiver are formed as a result of the actual communication patterns between the individual and the attachment figure. Similarly, Bretherton (1988) emphasizes that, in both childhood and adulthood, the caregiver's sensitivity to the individual's requests for attention, comfort, or encouragement is crucial in the development of working models. Ainsworth (Ainsworth, Bell, & Stayton, 1974) defines sensitive parental responsiveness as involving the parent being able to take the infant's perspective, notice the infant's goals, and respond empathically to those goals.

Bretherton (1988) argues that a secure relationship between an infant and his or her attachment figure is related to each partner's ability to engage in emotionally open, fluent, and coherent communication. This effect applies both to the communication *within* the attachment relationship and to the individual's communication *about* the relationship. In other words, insecure relationships are characterized by the caregiver being insensitive to the infant's signals within the relationship, as well as by the child being incoherent when talking about the attachment relationship at some later time.

According to Bretherton (1988), children whose mothers are insensitive to their signals continually receive implicit messages about the inadequacy of their communication; for example, that they cannot be understood or that their communications are unimportant. Bretherton emphasizes that insensitive responses are not necessarily mean or nasty, although they may be rejecting (at least by implication) or intrusive.

Grossmann and Grossmann (1984) identified three maternal conversational styles that they labeled as *tender* (high responsiveness, even attentiveness, generous soothing, calm tone), *lighthearted* (fast tempo, extreme variability in loudness and pitch, demanding, much laughing, often delayed responding), and *sober* (slow tempo, few short utterances, uneven responding, long reaction time). These conversational styles were related to independent ratings of maternal sensitivity and to the baby's tendency to vocalize. Infants whose mothers used the more intrusive and demanding light-hearted style are less likely than others to increase their vocalizing between 2 months and 10 months and were more likely to be insecure. The tender style was used by about half of the mothers of secure infants, but by only small percentages of mothers of insecure infants. The sober style was fairly common across all three attachment groups.

In an observational study of mother-child interaction, the greater sensitivity of the mothers of secure infants was shown in two ways (Escher-Graeub & Grossmann, 1983). First, these mothers were less likely than others to ignore signals from their infants; second, they were more likely to watch quietly when their children were playing happily and seemed not to need them, but to join in if their child needed help. Avoidant mothers tended to withdraw from their infants when they expressed negative feelings. Matas et al. (1978) found similar patterns for 2-year-old children engaged in a problem-solving task. Secure children sought help only when they needed it; their mothers respected their autonomy, but provided help when it was requested.

A further study by this group of researchers (Grossmann, Grossmann, & Schwan, 1986) involved analyzing the communication of mothers and infants during the Strange Situation episodes (see Chapter 1). Secure infants were more likely than avoidant infants to engage their mothers in direct communication (eye contact, vocalization, facial expression, showing and giving objects). Avoidant infants tended to engage their mothers in direct communication only when they were feeling happy.

Bretherton (1988) summarizes the findings of a number of studies of parent-child communication by describing the characteristics of the interactions between parents and children of the different attachment groups. Secure children and parents are able to communicate about attachment issues with ease and coherence and to accept each other's imperfections. Avoidant children and their parents defend against closeness by restricting the flow of ideas about attachment relationships; they seem aloof and nonempathic in their interactions with one another. Avoidant children also have a tendency to idealize both themselves and their parents, although they have difficulty giving concrete examples of this "ideal" behavior. As the name implies, anxious-ambivalent children tend to show ambivalent feelings toward their mothers during reunion. They also show preoccupation with attachment issues in adulthood, particularly where there is conflict.

Kobak and Duemmler (1994) see conversations between parents and children as the primary avenue through which individuals negotiate goal conflicts and maintain attachment relationships. Open communication of attachment goals should be enhanced in families where cooperative responses are expected; in such families, a history of responsiveness leads to working models involving positive views of self and other and facilitates the development of effective communication skills.

In support of this proposition, we noted earlier that secure babies engage in more direct communication. Mothers who ignore their children's signals about attachment needs may implicitly teach their children not to communicate such needs directly. On the other hand, mothers who accurately read and respond to their children's signals may teach their children to communicate attachment goals and needs directly.

With the development of language, children acquire the capacity to talk about their internal states and their attachment needs; this new skill expands the range of situations for secure base and safe haven behavior. Children can now have their attachment needs met and feel comforted in a symbolic way (e.g., by imagining the affectionate behaviors of an absent attachment figure), as well as by the actual presence of the attachment figure.

According to Kobak and Duemmler (1994), conversations between parents and children that increase the understanding of differences and lead to cooperation may become critical to attachment security in childhood and adolescence. Conversations are seen as crucial because they facilitate open lines of communication, enable participants to gain important new information about one another, and allow them to share and reflect on their goals and feelings. Conversations also provide an opportunity for updating inadequate or out of date working models. For effective and open communication to occur, the clear expression of one's own goals and feelings must be supplemented by a capacity to listen and to understand the partner's goals and feelings.

In the first instance, secure working models facilitate the development of conversational skills because the child's confidence in self and others leads to increased willingness and motivation to engage in conversations. As the secure child continues to try out conversational skills in this atmosphere of open communication, he or she learns that expressing emotions can be a constructive way to get one's needs met. In addition, over time, the child gains further confidence in using language to verbalize goals and feelings. The secure child may also have a greater capacity to attend to the caregiver's signals and goals without fear of a negative response, to accommodate to the wishes and needs of others, and to negotiate about issues and problems.

❧ Attachment, Communication, and Intimate Relationships

If communication is so important in the development of working models in the child, then communication in the close relationships of adults is also likely to be affected by attachment style. A number of researchers have explored the links between attachment and communication in romantic and marital relationships.

Pistole (1989) investigated the implications of attachment style for reports of conflict resolution in a sample of students involved in love relationships. She used Hazan and Shaver's (1987) three-group measure of attachment style and Rahim's (1983) Organizational Conflict Inventory. Rahim's measure is based on a two-dimensional model of approaches to conflict (Blake & Mouton, 1964); the dimensions are concern for self and concern for the relationship. As can be seen in Figure 5.2, aggression (domination) is high in concern for self and low in concern for the relation-

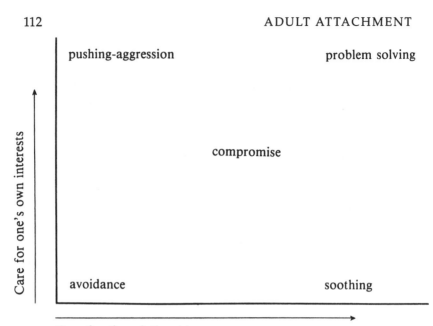

Figure 5.2. Two-Dimensional Model of Approaches to Conflict
SOURCE: Schaap et al. (1988).

ship, avoidance is low in concern for both self and relationship, soothing (obliging) is low in concern for self and high in concern for the relationship, and problem-solving (integrating) is high in concern for both self and relationship. Compromising is seen as midway on both dimensions; that is, moderate in concern for both self and relationship.

Pistole (1989) found that secure individuals were more likely to use an integrating strategy than those who were avoidant or anxious-ambivalent. Secure individuals also compromised more than anxious-ambivalents, whereas anxious-ambivalents were more likely to oblige the partner than were avoidants. These findings support the tendency for secure individuals to use more constructive strategies in dealing with conflict; that is, strategies that reflect concern both for their own interests and for enhancing the quality of the relationship.

The link between attachment style and self-disclosure was investigated by Mikulincer and Machshon (1991), using self-report

and behavioral methods. Secure and anxious-ambivalent individuals reported more self-disclosure than avoidant individuals. Secure individuals also showed the most flexibility (in
terms of the range of self-disclosure across various social situations) and the most reciprocity (in terms of the particular topics
discussed with partners).

Kobak and Hazan (1991) investigated the role of working
models in marital functioning. Spouses completed measures of
dyadic satisfaction and working models of attachment and
engaged in two interaction tasks: a standard problem-solving
interaction and a confiding task in which they shared a disappoint-
ment or loss unrelated to the marriage. Problem-solving discus-
sions were rated on two scales: rejection and support-validation.
Confiding interactions were rated for speaker's disclosure (the
extent to which the individual seemed confident that the partner
would understand) and the listener's acceptance of distress
(ability to accept the speaker's feelings of distress and help clarify
these feelings).

Kobak and Hazan (1991) were interested in both the security and
the accuracy of working models (with accuracy assessed in terms
of the level of agreement with the spouse about one's own working
models). Spouses with secure working models reported higher
marital adjustment than those with insecure working models.
Secure wives were less likely to be rejected by husbands during
problem solving, and secure husbands were less rejecting and
more supportive on the same task. In terms of partner effects,
wives of less secure husbands were more rejecting and less supportive than other wives, and husbands of secure wives listened
more effectively during the problem-solving task. Accuracy of
working models was related to marital adjustment as well as to
observers' ratings of communication in both the problem-solving
and the confiding task.

Given that attachment style is strongly linked with both communication and marital satisfaction, it has been suggested that the
link between attachment style and satisfaction may stem, in part,
from the ways in which the different attachment groups communicate. Feeney, Noller, and Callan (1994) explored the links between
attachment, communication, and relationship satisfaction using a

longitudinal design with young couples in the first 2 years of marriage. They used a two-factor measure of attachment involving scales of anxiety over relationships and comfort with closeness (see Chapter 3 of this volume) and measured three aspects of communication: the quality of communication in day-to-day interactions, self-reported conflict style, and nonverbal accuracy.

Quality of day-to-day interactions was assessed by having couples keep diaries of all their interactions with the partner over a 1-week period and rate the quality of those interactions on a number of scales. For husbands, comfort with closeness was positively related to ratings of involvement, recognition, disclosure, and satisfaction. For wives, anxiety over relationships was negatively related to ratings of involvement and satisfaction and positively related to ratings of domination and conflict. Thus, which dimension of attachment is most clearly related to quality of day-to-day communication depends on gender, with comfort with closeness having the strongest effect on communication for husbands and anxiety having the strongest effect for wives.

Conflict patterns were assessed with the Communication Patterns Questionnaire (Christensen & Sullaway, 1984), using the four factors of mutuality, coercion, destructive process, and postconflict distress, found by Noller and White (1990). Husbands who reported being comfortable with closeness were more likely to describe their conflicts with the partner as high in mutuality; husbands who were anxious about their relationships tended to report their conflicts as high in coercion, destructive process, and postconflict distress and low in mutuality. Anxious wives reported high levels of coercion and postconflict distress and low levels of mutuality. These results suggest that, in conflict situations, anxiety over basic relationship issues is related to destructive patterns of communication for both husbands and wives.

Nonverbal accuracy, or the extent to which spouses are able to understand one another's nonverbal messages, was assessed using a standard content paradigm involving ambiguous messages that could be positive, neutral, or negative, depending on the nonverbal behavior accompanying them. Husbands high in anxiety were low in accuracy for all three message types. Wives high in closeness were more accurate for both neutral and negative messages, but not for positive messages.

Overall, communication in the marital relationship was clearly linked to the two attachment dimensions of anxiety over relationships and comfort with closeness, although the effects varied with the gender of the spouse. Analyses over time showed that attachment scales predicted later relationship variables. Specifically, anxiety predicted later negative conflict patterns for wives and lower levels of decoding accuracy and relationship satisfaction for husbands; comfort with closeness predicted later decoding accuracy for wives. Quality of marital interaction, however, also predicted later attachment security for husbands. The latter finding supports the idea that working models of attachment may be revised on the basis of experience with intimate relationships.

The possibility that the link between attachment and satisfaction is mediated by communication patterns (as noted above) was also explored by Feeney, Noller, and Callan (1994). The results, however, provided little support for this hypothesis. Rather, the findings suggested that, in these early marriages, attachment and communication had independent effects on marital satisfaction.

Feeney (1994) assessed conflict patterns, attachment, and marital satisfaction in a large sample of couples at different stages of the marital life-cycle (married between 1 and 10 years, 11 to 20 years, more than 20 years). She found that secure individuals tended to be paired with secure spouses. Secure spouses were generally high in marital satisfaction; moreover, the combination of an anxious wife and a husband uncomfortable with closeness provided the least satisfactory relationship for both partners.

Mutual negotiation of conflict was the single most important predictor of satisfaction for both husbands and wives. The link between security of attachment and marital satisfaction was mediated by communication patterns for wives; in other words, the higher satisfaction reported by secure wives appears to be explained in terms of more constructive ways of communicating during conflict episodes. For husbands, conflict style only partially mediated the link between security of attachment and marital satisfaction, and anxiety over relationships explained variance in marital satisfaction over and above that related to the communication patterns.

⁊ Summary

In this chapter, we have examined more closely the concept of working models. Individual differences in attachment style are attributed to systematic differences in these underlying models of self and others, as formed through early attachment experiences and modified by subsequent relationship events. Working models include four interrelated components: memories of attachment-related experiences, beliefs and expectations of self and other in relation to attachment, attachment-related goals and needs, and strategies and plans for achieving those goals. These models affect relationships with others by shaping cognitive, emotional, and behavioral responses. Working models are relatively stable because they tend to operate automatically and because they may be self-perpetuating. Working models are most likely to change around significant life transitions, or as individuals reach new understandings of past attachment-related experiences through such processes as education or therapy. Bowlby (1969) argues that working models are formed as a result of the communication between the individual and the attachment figure, with the caregiver's sensitivity to the infant's signals being crucial to the development of security. Communication in adults' close relationships is also affected by attachment style. Secure individuals tend to use more constructive styles of dealing with conflict. In particular, anxiety about relationships seems to be an important predictor of behavior during conflict for both husbands and wives. There is some evidence that conflict patterns may mediate the relation between attachment and relationship satisfaction, although the findings are not consistent.

6

❦

Adult Attachment
Broadening the Picture

In previous chapters, we focused on the assessment of adult attachment, the functions of attachment behavior, and the implications of attachment style for communication and other aspects of relationship functioning. Our aim in this chapter is to present work that relates attachment style to other salient characteristics of the individual or to other important dimensions of behavior. Some of this work continues to focus on relationship issues: Specifically, we examine the proposition that romantic love involves the integration of several systems of behavior, and we explore issues concerning the links between gender, attachment style and relationship outcomes. Other studies that we discuss here have broadened the base of the attachment perspective by relating attachment style to constructs associated with, but clearly extending beyond, relationship behavior: namely, personality and well-being.

❧ Attachment as the Integration of Behavioral Systems

Consistent with Bowlby's (1969, 1973, 1980) ethological attachment theory, Shaver et al. (1988) argue that sexuality and caregiving are independent behavioral systems integrated with the attachment system in prototypical adult romantic love (see Chapter 2 of this volume). In other words, romantic love involves three key components: attachment, caregiving, and sexuality.

As we showed in Chapter 1, the attachment system appears very early in the course of the individual's development and it plays a vital role in the formation of mental models of self and others. For these reasons, the attachment system is likely to influence the expression of caregiving and sexuality and is seen as pivotal to the establishment and maintenance of romantic relationships.

It has also been suggested that the integration of these three components of romantic love follows a predictable developmental course (Hazan & Shaver, 1994). Specifically, attachment and caregiving increase in importance and intensity during the early years of a relationship, before leveling off; sexuality peaks in importance relatively early in the relationship, with subsequent fluctuations over time (see Figure 6.1).

What support is available for Hazan and Shaver's (1994) proposition that romantic relationships involve the integration of attachment, caregiving, and sexuality? Empirical studies provide considerable support for the importance of each of the proposed components of romantic love, considered separately. We have already discussed at some length the strong association between attachment style and relationship outcomes. The importance of caregiving in intimate bonds is supported by the finding that marital satisfaction can be predicted more strongly by an index of caregiving-care receiving than by measures of personality, material circumstances, and health (Kotler, 1985). Similarly, sexual

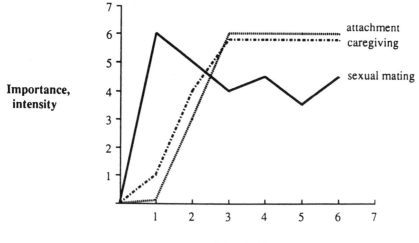

Figure 6.1. Developmental Course of the Three Components of Romantic Love

SOURCE: Hazan and Shaver (1994).

satisfaction is an acknowledged contributor to both relationship quality and stability (Sprecher & McKinney, 1993).

There is also growing support for links between attachment style and each of the other proposed components of romantic love. In a study of dating and married couples, Carnelley, Pietromonaco, and Jaffe (in press) assessed the link between attachment style and caregiving, together with the implications of these two variables for relationship satisfaction. Attachment style was defined by scales measuring fearful-avoidance and preoccupation, and caregiving was defined in terms of *beneficial care* (a composite scale based on items assessing reciprocal, selfless, and neglectful caregiving). Own security of attachment was linked with the provision of more beneficial care to romantic partners. Moreover, own attachment security, partner's attachment security, and provision of beneficial care all contributed to the prediction of relationship satisfaction.

Additional support for the link between attachment and caregiving comes from work by Kunce and Shaver (1994). These researchers developed self-report items to assess the quality of caregiving in intimate dyads, based on the literature on infant-caregiver bonds. Factor analysis of their measure revealed four scales: proximity (vs. distance), sensitivity (vs. insensitivity), cooperation (vs. control), and compulsive caregiving. In a student sample, these scales differentiated attachment groups as defined by a four-group measure. As expected, secure subjects reported high proximity and sensitivity, whereas dismissing subjects reported low proximity and sensitivity; both these groups reported a lack of compulsive caregiving. Consistent with their need for the approval of others, preoccupied and fearful subjects reported high compulsive caregiving but low sensitivity.

Support is also emerging for the link between attachment and sexuality. Brennan and Shaver (1995) found that avoidant individuals were more likely than secure individuals to engage in one-night stands and to endorse the idea that sex without love is pleasurable. Similarly, Feeney, Noller, and Patty (1993) found that avoidant individuals were more accepting of casual (uncommitted) sex than other attachment groups. In a diary study, these authors also found that female avoidants and male anxious-ambivalents were the least likely to report engaging in sexual intercourse during the course of the study. This finding suggests that gender and attachment style interact in their effects on sexual behavior; furthermore, the low level of intercourse reported by female avoidants is surprising given avoidants' greater acceptance of casual sex, and highlights the need to assess the effects of attachment style on both sexual attitudes and sexual behaviors.

Hazan, Zeifman, and Middleton (1994) present the most comprehensive study of the relations between attachment and the expression of sexuality. This study employed a sample of 100 adults who completed measures of attachment style and the frequency and enjoyment of various sexual behaviors. The results suggest that three distinct sexual styles can be identified, consistent with the three major attachment styles.

Secure individuals, for example, were less likely to get involved in one-night stands and in having sex outside the primary relationship, and were more likely to be involved in mutually initiated sex and to enjoy physical contact (whether sexually explicit or not). By contrast, avoidant individuals tended to report activities indicative of low psychological intimacy (one-night stands, extrarelationship sex, sex without love), as well as less enjoyment of physical contact. Anxious-ambivalent females reported involvement in exhibitionism, voyeurism, and domination-bondage; anxious-ambivalent males, on the other hand, appeared to be more sexually reticent. For both sexes, anxious-ambivalent attachment was associated with enjoyment of holding and caressing but not of more clearly sexual behaviors.

Although we know of no published empirical work integrating all three components of romantic bonds (attachment, caregiving, and sexuality), such work will undoubtedly be carried out. This integrative approach offers the promise of a comprehensive theory of romantic love. In particular, it may help clarify developmental changes in close relationships, especially at transition points. The transition to parenthood, for example, is likely to involve major upheaval in all three behavioral systems, as the dyadic relationship is expanded to include a third, highly dependent member; attachment groups may differ markedly in their responses to these changes.

ے Gender Differences and Similarities

No discussion of a theory of close relationships would be complete without a consideration of gender differences and similarities. Two questions are addressed here. The first question concerns gender differences in attachment patterns; that is, do men and women differ in attachment style? The second question concerns gender differences in the implications of attachment style for relationship functioning; that is, does endorsement of a particular attachment style (e.g., anxious-ambivalent) have different consequences for men and women? These two questions are logically independent: Endorsement of a particular attachment style may have different implications for men and women, even though the two genders may be equally likely to choose that style.

Gender Differences in Attachment Style

In the first empirical studies of adult attachment, Hazan and Shaver (1987) reported that gender was unrelated to endorsement of the secure, avoidant, and anxious-ambivalent attachment styles. This finding has been widely replicated by other researchers using the three-group categorical measure (e.g., Brennan et al., 1991; Feeney & Noller, 1990, 1992; Feeney et al., 1993). Furthermore, when a three-factor solution is forced from the set of individual statements making up the three-group measure, there are no gender differences on the resulting continuous measures of secure, avoidant, and anxious-ambivalent attachment (Carnelley & Janoff-Bulman, 1992).

Interestingly, these results are in accordance with studies of infant attachment, which reveal no gender differences in the prevalence of the major attachment styles. At the same time, the lack of gender differences in adult attachment styles may seem somewhat counterintuitive; the discomfort with intimacy that characterizes the description of avoidant attachment appears similar to the stereotype of male relationship behavior, whereas the clinging, fearful style associated with anxious-ambivalence appears similar to the stereotype of female relationship behavior.

In line with these stereotypes, categorical and continuous measures of Bartholomew's (Bartholomew & Horowitz, 1991) four attachment prototypes have yielded gender differences, as have multiple-item attachment scales. Responses to the categorical four-group measure reveal strong gender differences in endorsement of the two avoidant categories, with males being much more likely than females to endorse the dismissing style and less likely than females to endorse the fearful style (Brennan et al., 1991).

Gender differences in continuous measures of the four attachment styles are partially supportive of these results: Males obtain higher mean ratings of dismissing attachment, whereas females obtain higher mean ratings of preoccupied attachment (Bartholomew & Horowitz, 1991; Scharfe & Bartholomew, 1994). These gender differences are robust, being evident in interview ratings, self-reports, and partner reports. Hence it appears that the four-group model is more sensitive than the three-group model in identifying gender differences in attachment patterns.

Although the wide variety of multiple-item attachment scales makes it difficult to establish converging findings, there is evidence that for college and high school samples, males are more likely than females to see relationships as secondary to achievement (Feeney, Noller, & Hanrahan, 1994). This finding fits with Bartholomew's (Bartholomew & Horowitz, 1991; Scharfe & Bartholomew, 1994) reports that men are more dismissing of attachment than women.

At the same time, multiple-item scales provide little support for gender differences in preoccupation or anxiety. One of the studies by Collins and Read (1990) suggests weak support for females' greater anxiety, consistent with Bartholomew's (Bartholomew & Horowitz, 1991; Scharfe & Bartholomew, 1994) results for preoccupied attachment. Research using scales with similar item content (anxiety over relationships, preoccupation with relationships) has not found reliable gender differences, however (Feeney, 1994; Feeney, Noller, & Callan, 1994; Feeney, Noller, & Hanrahan, 1994).

Studies of multiple-item scales do point to females' greater comfort with intimacy. Wives, for example, report greater comfort with closeness than husbands (Feeney, 1994; Feeney, Noller, & Callan, 1994), together with greater willingness to rely on partner (Kobak & Hazan, 1991). Similarly, female high school students report less discomfort with closeness than males and greater confidence in self and others (Feeney, Noller, & Hanrahan, 1994). Females' greater comfort with intimacy can be understood in terms of socialization patterns, with females being encouraged to be more nurturing and more relationship oriented.

In summary, the original measure of adult attachment style appears to be unrelated to gender. By contrast, subsequent measures suggest that males are more dismissing of attachment and that, on some attachment measures, females show greater comfort with closeness and greater preoccupation with relationships.

Gender Differences in the Implications of Attachment Style

As we showed in Chapter 5, several researchers have assessed the implications of own and partner's attachment style for
relationship quality; they frequently note gender differences in the
pattern of results. Collins and Read (1990), for example, reported
that men's comfort with closeness (close) was the strongest predictor of their own and their partners' relationship evaluations, whereas women's fear of abandonment (anxiety) was the
strongest predictor of their own and their partners' relationship
evaluations.

In explaining these results, Collins and Read (1990) note that the
observed gender differences can be related to traditional sex-role
stereotypes. That is, women are socialized to value emotional
closeness, whereas men are socialized to value independence. For
both women and men, extreme conformity to these sex-role
stereotypes may be detrimental to relationship quality, particularly as perceived by the partner (Cancian, 1987). Hence, both
partners see their relationships negatively when the woman is
very anxious about relationship issues and the man is uncomfortable with intimacy (Collins & Read, 1990). We return to this explanation of gender differences later in this section.

The importance of men's comfort with intimacy is supported by
other researchers. Simpson (1990) found that, although men's
relationship evaluations were linked with self-reports of all three
attachment styles, the most consistent effects were for secure and
avoidant attachment; both of these scales assess comfort (or discomfort) with intimacy. Similarly, Kirkpatrick and Davis (1994)
note that men describing themselves as avoidant in attachment
provided relatively negative reports of their relationships.

Evidence of the importance of women's anxiety about relationship issues is equally compelling. Women's anxiety (measured in
various ways) has been linked with negative reports of the quality
of dating and marital relationships, as provided by both self and
partner (Feeney, 1994; Feeney, Noller, & Callan, 1994; Kirkpatrick
& Davis, 1994; Simpson, 1990).

Despite support for the negative effects of men's discomfort
with intimacy and women's anxiety about relationships, three

separate findings suggest that gender-linked implications of adult attachment are more complex than these results suggest. First, Feeney (1994) found that, in relatively short-term marriages, wives' anxiety interacted with husbands' comfort to predict satisfaction (see Chapter 3 of this volume). Mean scores indicated that wives' anxiety adversely affected satisfaction only in the presence of a husband low in comfort, whereas men's anxiety was generally detrimental to satisfaction irrespective of the wives' attachment style. The observed interaction is not inconsistent with the main effect of women's anxiety, as noted by Collins and Read (1990) and other researchers (and as evident in Feeney's own study); it does, however, suggest a different explanation of gender differences. Recall that Collins and Read propose that behavior that strongly confirms sex-role stereotypes may be detrimental to relationships. By contrast, Feeney's results suggest that the pervasive negative effect of husbands' anxiety may reflect *violation* of sex-role stereotypes; wives' anxiety, being stereotype confirming, is detrimental only when partners fail to provide high levels of comfort and support.

Second, a comprehensive longitudinal study of attachment in marriage (Feeney, Noller, & Callan, 1994) points to complex links between gender, attachment, and relationship functioning. Diary reports of day-to-day interactions supported previous research, in pointing to the negative effects of wives' anxiety and husbands' lack of comfort on measures of involvement and satisfaction with communication. By contrast, reports of communication patterns adopted during conflict pointed to the negative effects of anxiety for both men and women; it appears that anxiety over basic relationship issues is an important source of marital conflict, linked with mistrust, jealousy, and coercion. Measures of nonverbal accuracy revealed yet another pattern of findings: For these measures, negative effects were strongest for husbands' anxiety and wives' closeness. The reason for this pattern is not yet clear. It is possible that for husbands, anxiety is strongly linked with psychophysiological arousal, especially in conflict situations; such arousal may interfere with the demands of the nonverbal communication task (Gottman & Levenson, 1988; Noller, 1993).

Third, longitudinal data point to the need to distinguish between relationship quality and stability. As noted above, Kirkpatrick and Davis (1994) found that negative reports of relationship quality were given by avoidant men and by avoidant and anxious-ambivalent women. Nevertheless, the relationships of avoidant men and anxious women showed high stability. Why might this be? Anxious women may be very active in their efforts to maintain their relationships (women tend to act as the emotional caretakers of close relationships); in addition, anxious women tended to be paired with avoidant men, who would confirm their expectations of relationship partners. Similarly, avoidant men were paired with either secure or anxious females; these types of partners are likely to strive actively to maintain their relationships.

Together, these findings point to complex links between gender, attachment dimensions, and relationship outcomes. Further assessment of these links is required, with available data suggesting the need to include a range of specific communication measures, as well as more global indexes of relationship quality.

ᴥ Attachment and Personality

Early research into the correlates of adult attachment style established clear relations with self-esteem. Collins and Read (1990), for example, found that global self-esteem was positively correlated with comfort with closeness (close) and negatively correlated with anxiety about relationships (anxiety). Using the three-group categorical measure of attachment style, Feeney and Noller (1990) found that secure subjects reported higher personal and social self-esteem than both avoidant and anxious-ambivalent subjects; self-esteem in relation to family members was highest for secure subjects and lowest for anxious-ambivalents.

These results suggest that attachment style may be related to the dimension of personality that has been variously labeled as *neuroticism* and *negative affectivity* (Shaver & Hazan, 1993). Furthermore, established links between attachment style and measures of sociability, assertiveness, and interpersonal confidence (Bartholomew & Horowitz, 1991; Collins & Read, 1990; Feeney & Noller, 1990) suggest possible relations with the extraversion dimension of personality. These two dimensions of personality are the ones most frequently included in personality tests.

To explore the relations between attachment style and these basic dimensions of personality, Feeney, Noller, and Hanrahan (1994) administered measures of attachment style (the Attachment Style Questionnaire) and personality (the Junior Eysenck Personality Questionnaire) to a sample of students in the early years of high school. Multivariate analyses revealed theoretically meaningful associations between the two sets of variables: Neuroticism was strongly linked with the attachment dimensions of preoccupation with relationships and need for approval, and extraversion was strongly positively linked with confidence in self and others and negatively linked with relationships as secondary to achievement and discomfort with closeness.

A more detailed analysis of the relations between attachment style and personality measures was conducted by Shaver and Brennan (1992). These researchers related categorical and continuous measures of secure, avoidant, and anxious-ambivalent attachment to the so-called Big Five dimensions of personality: neuroticism, extraversion, openness to experience, agreeableness, and conscientiousness. In terms of the categorical measure, attachment groups were differentiated by their scores on neuroticism, extraversion, and agreeableness. Secure subjects obtained lower scores on neuroticism and higher scores on extraversion than both insecure groups; they also obtained higher scores on agreeableness than did avoidant subjects. Furthermore, the same pattern of results was found for correlations between the personality scales and continuous measures of the three attachment styles (Shaver & Brennan, 1992).

The presence of reliable associations between measures of attachment style and personality is not surprising, given that attachment theory can be seen as a general theory of personality development (Bowlby, 1980). Extreme overlap between the two sets of measures would be problematic, however, because it would suggest that attachment style is redundant with basic dimensions of personality. Hence, the results of the studies reported in this section are relevant to the conceptualization of attachment styles.

The results reported by Feeney, Noller, and Hanrahan (1994) point to very strong links between measures of attachment and personality; by contrast, the correlations in Shaver and Brennan's (1992) study were only modest in size. These contrasting results may stem from characteristics of the samples and the attachment measures used in these studies. Feeney, Noller, and Hanrahan employed a sample of young adolescents and a measure designed to be suitable for those with little or no experience of romantic relationships; hence, responses to this measure are likely to reflect relatively general attitudes to self, others, and social relationships. For subjects with greater experience of romantic relationships, reported feelings about closeness are likely to be more clearly differentiated from general dimensions of personality.

Another aspect of Shaver and Brennan's (1992) study suggests that attachment measures, rather than being redundant with personality dimensions, make a unique contribution to the study of individual differences. Specifically, these researchers compared the utility of attachment and personality measures as predictors of relationship quality and relationship outcomes. The results indicated that most relationship variables assessed by these researchers (relationship status, satisfaction, and commitment) were better predicted by the relationship-specific attachment measures than by the more general personality measures.

Attachment and Well-Being

As we discussed in the previous section, secure attachment has been clearly linked with high self-esteem and with low levels of negative affectivity. In addition, the studies examined in Chapter 4 demonstrate that securely attached individuals respond more constructively to stressful situations of various kinds. Together with the robust relations between secure attachment and more stable and satisfying intimate relationships, these results suggest that attachment style should have important implications for individual adjustment and well-being.

The link between attachment and general adjustment has been investigated primarily with adolescent samples. (This focus on young samples may reflect the salience of issues concerning adolescent adjustment; it may also reflect the fact that with older samples, researchers can focus on outcomes that relate more directly to involvement in established intimate relationships.) Greenberg and colleagues (Armsden & Greenberg, 1987; Greenberg, Siegel, & Leitch, 1983), for example, used self-report measures (the Inventory of Parent and Peer Attachment and a precursor to this instrument) to assess the quality of the adolescent's relationships with attachment figures. These researchers showed that quality of attachment to parents (a composite score reflecting levels of trust, communication, and alienation) predicted self-esteem and life satisfaction beyond that accounted for by attachment to peers. Quality of attachment to parents was also related to emotional functioning, with high quality of attachment predicting lower levels of anxiety, anger, depression, resentment, and guilt.

Rice (1990) conducted a meta-analysis of studies linking adolescent attachment with indexes of adjustment (academic, social, and emotional). This meta-analysis was based on 30 studies published between 1975 and 1990. Results indicated a reliable positive association between attachment and measures of social and emotional adjustment, but no reliable association with measures of academic adjustment. Effect sizes (which indicate the strength of association between attachment and adjustment) were generally modest. In considering the limited effect sizes, however, bear in mind that most of the studies reviewed by Rice predate the work of Hazan and Shaver (1987). Accordingly, most assessed attachment using a single index of quality of attachment to parents, a practice that fails to consider the multidimensional nature of attachment. (An exception is the study by Kobak and Sceery, 1988, which compared the adjustment of secure, dismissing, and preoccupied attachment groups; see Chapter 2 of this volume.)

A number of researchers have focused specifically on the link between attachment and depression. For example, Richman and Flaherty (1987) report a 7-month longitudinal study of first-year medical students. Attachment to parents was defined in terms of retrospective reports of maternal and paternal care and over-protection during subjects' childhood, using the Parental Bonding Instrument (Parker, Tupling, & Brown, 1979). Their results support the link between the quality of early attachments and later levels of depression: Depression at Time 2 was related positively to Time 1 ratings of maternal and paternal overprotection and negatively to Time 1 ratings of maternal and paternal care. This study is one of several in which attachment to parents, as assessed by the Parental Bonding Instrument, has been related to later levels of depression (see Parker, 1994, for a summary of this research).

Strahan (1995) provides a more complex analysis of the association between attachment and depression, proposing that the effects of early attachment on depression may be mediated in part by the quality of current attachment relationships. Using an older subject sample, Strahan found some evidence of direct links between early attachments and later depression, in accordance with the work of Richman and Flaherty (1987); depression was directly linked with reports of childhood overprotection from the parent of the opposite sex (see Figure 6.2). Support was also obtained, however, for the proposed mediational model. Specifically, the effect of early maternal care on depression was mediated by degree of comfort with closeness in current attachment relationships. Hence, it appears that the inverse association between maternal care and adult depression is largely explained by the fact that subjects reporting high levels of maternal care during childhood are able to develop closer and more supportive peer relationships in the present.

This finding is consistent with the proposition that individual development is marked by continuity and coherence (Sroufe, 1979, 1988). That is, although the individual's behavior patterns alter with the course of development, these patterns show qualitative similarities over time. Thus the young child who displays the characteristics of secure attachment to the mother (actively seeking physical contact with her and deriving comfort from such contact) manifests social competence in terms of intimate and supportive relationships with peers at a later time. Early security of attachment may not directly influence later outcomes, however; rather, it may provide a context in which subsequent develop-

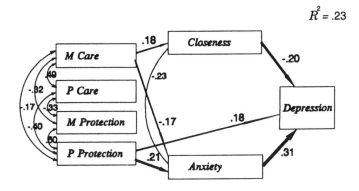

College Females *(N = 172)*

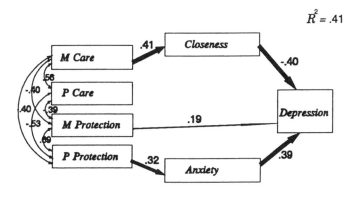

College Males *(N = 75)*

Figure 6.2. Relations Among Parental Bonding, Current Attachment, and Depression

SOURCE: Strahan (1995).

mental issues are more likely to be effectively addressed. In this way, both early and later experience play key roles in the individual's development (Sroufe, 1988). (This view is also consistent with the theoretical model of relationship functioning proposed by Carnelley et al., 1994, in which the effect of childhood experiences on later relationship functioning may be mediated by current attachment style or by levels of depression.)

Evidence of the broad ramifications of attachment style for the individual adjustment of adult subjects is provided by Hazan and Shaver (1990; this research is discussed in Chapter 4 in relation to the link between love and work). This study included a measure of well-being that yielded five major factors: loneliness and depression, anxiety, hostility, psychosomatic illness, and physical illness. Attachment groups, as defined by the three-group forced-choice measure, differed reliably on all five dimensions of well-being, with secure subjects in each case reporting higher well-being than either avoidant or anxious-ambivalent subjects.

In addition to the studies described above, most of which employed nonclinical groups, the link between attachment and adjustment has been investigated using clinical samples. Although a detailed review of this work is beyond the scope of the present volume, it is important to note that theoretical models and empirical research in this area are becoming increasingly sophisticated. Clinicians and researchers have recognized that adjustment problems typically reflect a developmental process in which both early and current life experiences are implicated.

In developing his model of risk factors for suicidal behavior, for example, Adam (1994) argues that negative attachment experiences early in life are a predisposing factor to such behavior. Furthermore, the internal working models that the individual develops, based on those early experiences, influence his or her capacity to form and maintain relationships with subsequent partners. This capacity is likely to be reflected in current relationship experiences, such as rejection by relationship partners, which may then serve as precipitating factors in suicidal behavior. Adam's theoretical model also takes account of contributing factors (e.g., the intake of alcohol) that may influence the expression of predisposing or precipitating factors, and protective factors (e.g., the availability of other caregivers) that may mitigate against the effects of adverse experiences. This theoretical model is also consistent with Sroufe's (1988) concept of continuity of individual adaptation, by which the individual's development is affected by both early and later experience; as noted above, early attachment security provides a context in which later developmental issues are likely to be resolved more effectively.

The studies discussed in this section document the association between secure attachment and subjective well-being. The important goal remaining for researchers in this area is to explain the mechanisms that underlie this association. A decade ago, West and colleagues (West, Livesley, Reiffer, & Sheldon, 1986) suggested that attachment may influence the onset of psychiatric illness in three ways: by giving rise to a nonspecific vulnerability to stress that predisposes to the onset of symptoms; by influencing the individual's ability to establish and use social networks; and by influencing appraisals of, and responses to, life events. Although researchers have begun to relate attachment measures to symptom reports, to social interaction patterns, and to responses to stressful events, little real advance has been made in comparing these factors as explanatory mechanisms for the link between attachment and well-being. Research of this kind is needed before attachment theory can be seen as a truly integrative theory of close relationships.

✖ Summary

The studies discussed in this chapter point to the wide-ranging implications of attachment style. Shaver and Hazan (1994) propose that the attachment system influences the expression of caregiving and sexuality, as manifested in romantic love. Further empirical testing of this proposition is required, but preliminary results support the utility of this perspective in providing a comprehensive explanation of love relationships. Although gender differences in attachment style are relatively weak (with the exception of males' greater endorsement of dismissing attachment), there is substantial evidence that the effects of attachment style on relationship outcomes are gender specific; in particular, it appears that these effects may be moderated by gender role stereotypes. Reliable links have been established between attachment style and basic dimensions of personality. These links are generally modest in size, however, and attachment style plays a unique role in predicting relationship functioning. The broader implications of attachment security for individual adjustment are supported by studies of emotional adjustment and subjective well-being and by research into clinical problems such as suicidal behavior.

7

❦

Applications and Future Directions

Bowlby's (1969, 1973, 1980) work on the nature of infant-mother bonds has clearly been a major force in the discipline of psychology. Ainsworth (1992) sums up the contribution of this work by declaring that attachment theory "has had a stronger impact on American psychology than any other theory of personality development since Sigmund Freud" (p. 668). Not surprisingly, then, an impressive array of research findings now support the principles of infant attachment theory.

In essence, this body of research focuses on the caregiving experiences required to meet children's emotional needs. As such, attachment theory and research have vital implications for practical questions concerning the care of young children. We noted in Chapter 1 that, following Bowlby's (1969, 1973, 1980) work, dramatic changes have taken place in the care of hospitalized and institutionalized children. Current practices surrounding the birth experience, for example, are designed to minimize physical separation of the parents from the new infant and from older children within the family. More generally, hospital treatment procedures and visiting schedules are increasingly based on the recognition that childhood separation from parents is stressful and has the potential to disrupt family relationships.

Ironically, despite the increasing emphasis on minimizing parent-child separations, economic and social conditions now strongly encourage both mothers and fathers to work outside the home. These pressures have fueled an ongoing debate concerning the possible negative effects of certain child care arrangements on the adjustment of children and families. Although this debate continues, some tentative conclusions seem to be emerging: It is important for parents to be reasonably available to their children, and it is also important that any alternative child care arrangements involve consistent and responsive caregiving.

At this point in time, it is more difficult to evaluate the contribution that will ultimately be made by adult attachment theory and research. One point is immediately apparent: The concept that adults' close relationships can be understood in terms of attachment principles has generated a body of research that is growing at a phenomenal rate. This rapid growth is reflected in a number of indexes that chart the development of this research area in the years following the publication of Hazan and Shaver's (1987) studies. For example, citation indexes show that by late 1995, almost 200 authors had already cited these ground-breaking studies. Similarly, the importance of this topic can be seen by the fact that in 1990, 10% of the papers presented at the International Conference on Personal Relationships focused on adult attachment; 2 years later, this figure had risen to 16%. In addition, since the recent (1994) inception of the *Personal Relationships* journal, studies of adult attachment have accounted for 18% of submissions to that journal and for 20% of the accepted papers.

It is also becoming clear that adult attachment theory will be useful in addressing a number of issues central to the study of close relationships, such as interpersonal attraction, compatibility, and conflict. In terms of interpersonal attraction, for example, the attachment perspective proposes that attraction results from one person's seeing the possibility of another person's meeting attachment, caregiving, or sexual needs (Hazan & Shaver, 1994). This proposition may not be easy to test empirically because it requires that the researcher take account of the different types of needs that may be fulfilled within romantic relationships. Nevertheless, this approach represents an advance over much previous research into interpersonal attraction, which has tended to focus on the simple identification of factors implicated in the attraction process (Hazan & Shaver, 1994).

Questions concerning compatibility between relationship partners can also be addressed within the attachment framework. The perceived quality of an attachment relationship may be largely dependent on the extent to which the partner is available and responsive to one's needs (Hazan & Shaver, 1994). At the normative level, the emphasis of attachment theory on perceived availability and responsiveness helps highlight the importance of trust within interpersonal relationships.

Individual differences in attachment history are also likely to be relevant to compatibility issues. An individual who has experienced inconsistent caregiving, for example, may have unmet attachment needs that are of prime importance but that may hinder the development of open and effective communication with a partner. Such an individual may also remain in a relationship with an "incompatible" partner despite the associated conflict, because of the nature of his or her expectations of personal relationships. As we have discussed at various points throughout this book, research into adult attachment has already told us quite a lot about patterns of attachment pairings and about the implications of these pairings for relationship quality and stability.

Conflict is another topic that is central to the study of close relationships and that has been addressed explicitly within the attachment perspective. All partners in close relationships experience some conflict; attachment theory helps us understand the sources of such conflict, together with individual differences in handling conflict. The evidence to date suggests that the anxiety over relationships' attachment dimension (related to the anxious-ambivalent or preoccupied style) is of particular importance here. Individuals high in anxiety over relationships report more relationship conflict; this finding suggests that much of the conflict occurring in these relationships is driven by basic insecurity over issues of love, loss, and abandonment. Interestingly, evidence also suggests that attachment style is more closely associated with responses to such relationship-centered conflict than to conflict over more concrete issues. It is important to note that those who are anxious about their relationships seem to engage in more destructive ways of dealing with conflict; in this way, their coercive and distrusting responses are likely to bring about the very outcomes they fear most.

Research into these topics is likely to have practical implications, particularly for therapists dealing with marital and family problems. First, as noted above, the attachment perspective sheds new light on the possible causes of marital conflict and the dynamics that may arise in relationships involving particular combinations of attachment styles. In addition, attachment theory and research highlight the important function of working models of attachment in guiding individuals' expectations and behavior in close relationships. This perspective suggests that therapists may play an active role in helping clients with negative attachment histories revise their working models; this goal may be achieved either through the therapeutic relationship itself or through cognitive-behavior therapy that challenges those existing working models.

In relation to therapeutic interventions, the attachment perspective has been used to study the clinical problems of adult subjects. We referred to some examples of this work in previous chapters (e.g., in considering the link between attachment style and measures of well-being, we mentioned research into depression and suicidal behavior). In addition, the argument that therapists may play an active role in helping clients revise negative working models of attachment is developed in some detail by Sperling and Lyons (1994). These authors outline the various kinds of therapeutic interventions dealing with "mental representations"; that is, with the enduring network of expectations, affects, and memories associated with clients' personal relationships. Some of these interventions focus quite explicitly on changing mental representations. Because mental representations influence attachment-related perceptions and behavior, such changes should affect the experience of current close relationships, leading to further modification of representations.

✎ Theoretical Issues

Although it seems clear that the attachment perspective will continue to shed new light on the nature and course of romantic relationships, there are a number of important controversies within the area. These controversies are highlighted in a recent volume of *Psychological Inquiry*, in which several researchers in the area comment on a target article outlining the attachment framework for research on close relationships (Hazan & Shaver, 1994). Some of the recurring theoretical issues raised in this volume are as follows. Do attachment styles reflect parenting or infant temperament? Are attachments singular or multiple? Are attachment patterns properties of individuals or of relationships? When do attachment styles become stable and how stable are they?

In this concluding chapter, it is important to consider these key questions, at least briefly. It should be noted, however, that each of these questions has also been raised in earlier sections of the book. In addition, some of these questions are closely interrelated, and hence one question cannot be thoroughly answered without reference to another.

As we noted in Chapter 1, the relative importance of parenting and infant temperament as determinants of attachment quality continues to be a source of debate. Although some studies have supported the role of infant temperament, the evidence for the importance of caregiving experiences is at least equally strong. As Hazan and Shaver (1994) point out, the importance of caregiver behavior has been convincingly demonstrated using an experimental design. Specifically, Van den Boom (1990) randomly assigned 100 babies who had been identified as temperamentally difficult to an experimental or control condition. The experimental condition involved mothers being trained to respond to their infants' needs in a sensitive manner. Approximately 3 months later, 68% of the infants in the experimental group were assessed as securely attached, compared with only 28% of those in the control group. We also noted that research into the relative importance of parenting and infant temperament has become increasingly complex, with comprehensive studies providing some evidence that parenting variables and infant temperament may interact to predict attachment style.

In terms of the number of attachments, the literature on infant attachments suggests that infants and children do form multiple attachments, but that these relationships are not all of equal importance to the child. Rather, the multiple attachments are thought to be hierarchically arranged, with the primary attachment figure (usually the mother) at the top of the hierarchy. Fathers and older siblings can also serve as important attachment figures, as can other individuals who consistently care for the child (nannies, grandparents, etc.). Similarly, in adulthood, a peer (usually a sexual partner) assumes the role of primary attachment figure, although other people may also be used as sources of comfort and security. Hazan and Zeifman (1994) chart the processes involved in the development of peer attachments in late adolescence. In addition, Collins and Read's (1994) work on the structure of working models helps clarify how a hierarchy of attachment figures is represented cognitively and how we might predict which part of the attachment network will be activated in a given situation.

As noted above, questions have also been raised concerning the stability of attachment styles, and the conceptualization of attachment styles as properties of individuals or properties of relationships. Attachment theorists (beginning with Bowlby) recognize that expectations concerning attachment relationships, as manifested in attachment styles, develop gradually throughout childhood and adolescence. Theorists also recognize that the stability of attachment style depends on the stability of the social environment, as supported by a large number of empirical studies. Similarly, adult attachment researchers widely accept that early working models of attachment may be modified by subsequent experiences that disconfirm expectations; such experiences may take place in therapeutic relationships (as noted earlier) or in relationships with intimate partners.

Closely tied to the stability issue are questions about whether attachment styles represent a trait of the individual or whether they vary with different relationship partners. Kirkpatrick and Hazan (1994) report that attachment styles are more stable than relationship status across a 4-year period. More important, however, we argue that the traits versus relationships controversy is based, to a large degree, on a false dichotomy. It is almost certain that responses to self-report measures of adult attachment reflect both influences; that is, relatively enduring characteristics of the individual, together with aspects of current relationship functioning. Furthermore, our enduring expectations of relationships, as embodied in working models, are likely to become translated into the reality of relationship functioning. Specifically, these expectations may be fulfilled by the way we choose relationship partners or by the way in which we behave within a relationship.

In summing up the crucial theoretical issues in this area, we first need to reiterate that adult attachment researchers have never claimed that adult attachment patterns reflect only patterns of maternal caregiving experienced during infancy, or that infant attachment styles are fixed for life, or that subsequent relationship experiences have no major effect on working models or attachment styles. Nevertheless, some questions related to these issues are important and require further research. For example, it is important for researchers to come to some agreement concerning the extent to which adult attachment styles are stable; this issue is likely to be a complex one, in which factors such as the type of attachment measure and the type of subject sample need to be considered. It is also important for researchers to explore much more fully the effects of various kinds of relationship experiences on the stability of attachment style. This issue can best be addressed by relatively long-term longitudinal studies in which individuals are followed up repeatedly within a given relationship or followed up as they move through the course of relationship formation and dissolution.

☜ Methodological Issues

Methodological issues have also been prominent in this area and have centered particularly on problems of conceptualization and measurement. Clearly, a key development has been the expanded four-group model of adult attachment proposed by Bartholomew (1990; Bartholomew & Horowitz, 1991). One of the attractions of this model is the fact that it is firmly grounded in theory, being based directly on Bowlby's concept of working models of self and others. There is also substantial empirical support for the four-group model; for example, the two types of avoidant attachment proposed by Bartholomew seem to show distinct patterns of interpersonal behavior.

In general, irrespective of the particular theoretical model of attachment style, there has been a move away from categorical to continuous measures (or to a combination of these two approaches). Continuous measures allow for a more complete description of subjects' attachment patterns, and tend to be less strongly influenced by researchers' preconceived notions concerning the number and nature of the various attachment groups.

Similarly, some data suggest that interview procedures may offer advantages over the various self-report questionnaires in terms of measuring attachment style; for example, interviews appear to provide data that are more stable over time (Scharfe & Bartholomew, 1994). Nevertheless, such measures are clearly time consuming to work with, and this feature may limit the size of the samples that can be studied.

Important divisions in the attachment area cut across the distinction between questionnaire and interview methodologies. Specifically, there has tended to be a division between social psychologists (following the work of Hazan and Shaver and of Bartholomew) and developmental psychologists (following the work of Ainsworth, Main, and others). These two schools have tended to develop their work in parallel, and sometimes with little integration. In addition, the two schools focus on different aspects of attachment, ask different questions, and measure different constructs. The developmental approach, as reflected in the Adult Attachment Interview, is based on extensive questioning about childhood relationships with parents; furthermore, this measure aims to assess not only the content of individuals' responses but also their level of defensiveness about these early relationships. The social approach, on the other hand, whether using self-reports or interview methods, focuses primarily on the quality of current romantic relationships. Hence the measures used by the two sets of researchers should not be seen as interchangeable in any way.

In addition to measurement issues, we see other issues in researching adult attachment as very important. First, there is the question of sampling. Many of the early studies in this area tended to focus on the traditional convenience sample of college students. One of the problems associated with this approach is that most of these subjects are quite young and hence may have relatively little experience of romantic relationships. The use of such participants raises important questions concerning the extent to which findings can be generalized to more representative samples, given that these subjects should certainly not be considered experts on love and relationships. Recent studies of adult attachment and marriage have helped redress this imbalance; these studies also highlight the fact that the attachment characteristics of the sample (broadly speaking, the overall degree of security) appear to vary with the relationship status of the participants.

Although the adult attachment area has clearly made many important advances since its recent beginnings, some research developments stand out as being particularly exciting. Jacobvitz, for example, conducted a longitudinal study in which three generations of females (grandmothers, mothers, and their first-born daughters) were assessed using a combination of interview and observational methods (Jacobvitz & Burton, 1994). This study focused on the relationships of new mothers with their own mothers and the implications of these relationships for the quality of care given to infant daughters. In addition, Jacobvitz is currently conducting a longitudinal study of couples undergoing the transition to parenthood; this study was designed to assess how couples' representations of their parents during childhood relate to the quality of their marriages and to the quality of care provided to their children. Such research has the potential to clarify how the "network of family relationships is carried forward to the next generation" (Jacobvitz & Burton, 1994, p.8).

Another exciting development has been the study of cognitive processes associated with working models. Baldwin and colleagues, for example, investigated attachment style differences in expectations of interactions with relationship partners (Baldwin, Fehr, Keedian, Seidel, & Thompson, 1993). A lexical decision task was used in which subjects were shown strings of letters and asked to identify each as a word or a nonword. Baldwin et al. were particularly interested in how different attachment styles (secure vs. avoidant) responded to positive and negative outcome words set in the context of interpersonal relationships. An example of a negative outcome is the sentence "If I depend on my partner, then my partner will. . . . " followed by the target word "leave." On some trials, however, target words were not set in an interpersonal context. Overall, targets were recognized as words more quickly when set in an interpersonal context, but this effect applied only to stimuli consistent with subjects' expectations of relationships. Specifically, the interpersonal context was associated with faster recognition of positive outcome words by secure subjects and of negative outcome words by avoidant subjects. These findings support the concept that interpersonal expectations, as reflected in attachment style, affect the way that social information is processed.

ⱥ Future Directions

As we have noted, researchers into adult attachment need to address a number of major theoretical and research issues. In addition to these issues, we see a number of more specific points as important for researchers to consider. These points reflect limitations in our understanding of key attachment processes.

First, we are still a long way from fully understanding the link between the patterns of relating that individuals experience with their caregivers and the expectations they later have for their own romantic relationships. For example, how does the avoidant individual, who is likely to have been subjected to rejection, distancing, and so on, come to expect that relationship partners will demand closeness? Some researchers have argued that, whereas the matching between parent and child attachment styles is likely to be guided by identification (Bowlby, 1973), the matching between romantic partners may reflect self-verification processes (i.e., our tendency to prefer others who confirm our expectations of ourselves in relation to others; see Pietromonaco & Carnelley, 1994). In this way, for example, an avoidant individual may become involved with a preoccupied partner, who confirms his or her beliefs that others demand closeness. Although this explanation seems plausible, it is not clear how or when the process of self-verification becomes relevant to partner matching.

Similarly, although it is frequently stated that different attachment styles involve different relationship goals, we do not fully understand what it is that individuals from the various attachment groups actually want from their relationships. For example, what do avoidant adults want in a relationship? Do they want someone who respects their need for distance? Or do they want someone who, by clinging and dependent behavior, confirms the expectation that relationship partners will demand closeness (i.e., a self-verification effect)? If the former applies (i.e., if avoidant individuals want someone who respects their need for distance), which type of partner best fulfills this wish? Is it a secure partner, who prefers closeness but can accept the avoidant individual's needs for distance? Or is it an avoidant partner, who is likewise motivated to maintain interpersonal distance?

Distinctions may also need to be made between what the members of particular attachment groups expect from relationships, what they would ideally like, and what they tend to end up with. Furthermore, there may be a difference between what they report they would like and what will actually be satisfying to them. For instance, we know from previous research that the combination of an avoidant male and an anxious-ambivalent female is stable but not necessarily satisfying (Kirkpatrick & Davis, 1994). Hence, it appears that certain insecure individuals may get hooked into relationships that are stable but quite conflicted.

As we mentioned earlier, there is a need for more longitudinal studies that follow couples over the course of long-term relationships. Such studies will enable researchers to look at the effect of particular attachment combinations and to see whether individuals in ongoing relationships change their attachment style over time. Equally important, there is a need to study longitudinally those individuals who move from relationship to relationship. In this way, we can begin to assess the link between stability of attachment style and specific relationship events.

Finally, we see a need to distinguish between the *core* aspects of attachment style and the *correlates* of attachment style. For instance, various researchers have advocated defining new attachment groups marked by particular features (e.g., controlling behavior, anger). Although questions concerning the number of major attachment groups have not necessarily been finally resolved, we need to ask whether additional attachment groups must be proposed to understand individual differences in variables such as anger. Alternatively, features such as anger may be more appropriately seen as correlates of previously defined attachment styles or attachment dimensions. By contrast, variables such as trust, dependence, confidence, comfort with closeness, and anxiety about relationships are clearly central to the attachment construct, as defined by descriptions of both infant and adult attachment styles. Note that similar issues of definition have plagued research into other aspects of close relationships, such as relationship satisfaction.

Throughout this volume we have explored the major directions of research into adult attachment processes over the years since the appearance of Hazan and Shaver's (1987) seminal article. Great progress has been made in our understanding of these processes. It has become clear that a major feature of the attachment perspective on close relationships is the breadth of its application: It highlights the universal nature of attachment behavior, but also helps explain how individual differences in relationship behavior are shaped by both early and subsequent social experiences. The formative role of early experience is in accord with the implicit theories of love espoused by many lay persons. For example, one of our subjects, when asked to describe his current relationship, spontaneously offered the following observation:

My partner is extremely affectionate, which suits me down to the ground. I've always, always craved affection all my life, mainly through parental—bad parental—relationships. So, I don't know, but I put it down to that—and she's the only person I've ever gone out with that's actually given me the affection I've wanted.

Despite the advances in our understanding of adult attachment processes, we have also tried to show that many questions still need to be answered. We will have achieved our goal if we have increased your interest in attachment issues and have encouraged some of you to consider research that will address these important questions.

References

Adam, K. S. (1994). Suicidal behavior and attachment: A developmental model. In M. B. Sperling & W. H. Berman (Eds.), *Attachment in adults: Theory, assessment, and treatment* (pp. 275-298). New York: Guilford.

Ainsworth, M. D. S. (1979). Infant-mother attachment. *American Psychologist, 34,* 932-937.

Ainsworth, M. D. S. (1982). Attachment: Retrospect and prospect. In C. M. Parkes & J. Stevenson-Hinde (Eds.), *The place of attachment in human behavior* (pp. 3-30). New York: Basic Books.

Ainsworth, M. D. S. (1985). Attachments across the life span. *Bulletin of the New York Academy of Medicine, 61,* 792-812.

Ainsworth, M. D. S. (1989). Attachments beyond infancy. *American Psychologist, 44,* 709-716.

Ainsworth, M. D. S. (1992). John Bowlby (1907-1990): Obituary. *American Psychologist, 47,* 668.

Ainsworth, M. D. S., Bell, S. M., & Stayton, D. (1974). Infant-mother attachment and social development. In M. P. Richards (Ed.), *The introduction of the child into the social world* (pp. 99-135). London: Cambridge University Press.

Ainsworth, M. D. S., Blehar, M. C., Waters, E., & Wall, S. (1978). *Patterns of attachment: A study of the strange situation.* Hillsdale, NJ: Lawrence Erlbaum.

Armsden, G. C., & Greenberg, M. T. (1987). The inventory of parent and peer attachment: Individual differences and their relationship to psychological well-being in adolescence. *Journal of Youth and Adolescence, 16,* 427-453.

Baldwin, M. W., & Fehr, B. (1995). On the instability of attachment style ratings. *Personal Relationships, 2,* 247-261.

Baldwin, M. W., Fehr, B., Keedian, E., Seidel, M., & Thomson, D. W. (1993). An exploration of the relational schemata underlying attachment styles: Self-report and lexical decision approaches. *Personality and Social Psychology Bulletin, 19,* 746-754.

Bartholomew, K. (1990). Avoidance of intimacy: An attachment perspective. *Journal of Social and Personal Relationships, 7,* 147-178.

Bartholomew, K., & Horowitz, L. M. (1991). Attachment styles among young adults: A test of a four-category model. *Journal of Personality and Social Psychology, 61,* 226-244.

Bates, J. E., & Bayles, K. (1988). Attachment and the development of behavior problems. In J. Belsky & T. Nezworski (Eds.), *Clinical implications of attachment* (pp. 253-299). Hillsdale, NJ: Lawrence Erlbaum.

Bates, J. E., Maslin, C. A., & Frankel, K. A. (1985). Attachment security, mother-child interaction, and temperament as predictors of behavior-problem ratings at age three years. *Monographs of the Society for Research in Child Development, 50*(1&2), 167-193.

Belsky, J., & Nezworski, T. (1988). Clinical implications of attachment. In J. Belsky & T. Nezworski (Eds.), *Clinical implications of attachment* (pp. 3-17). Hillsdale, NJ: Lawrence Erlbaum.

Belsky, J., & Rovine, M. (1987). Temperament and attachment security in the strange situation: An empirical rapprochement. *Child Development, 58,* 787-795.

Blake, R. R., & Mouton, J. S. (1964). *The managerial grid.* Houston: Gult.

Bower, G. H., & Cohen, P. R. (1982). Emotional influences in memory and thinking: Data and theory. In M. S. Clark & S. T. Fiske (Eds.), *Affect and cognition: The 17th Annual Carnegie Symposium on Cognition.* Hillsdale, NJ: Lawrence Erlbaum.

Bowlby, J. (1969). *Attachment and loss* (Vol. 1). New York: Basic Books.

Bowlby, J. (1973). *Attachment and loss* (Vol. 2). New York: Basic Books.

Bowlby, J. (1979). *The making and breaking of affectional bonds.* London: Tavistock.

Bowlby, J. (1980). *Attachment and loss* (Vol. 3). New York: Basic Books.

Bowlby, J. (1984). *Attachment and loss* (Vol. 1, 2nd ed.). Harmondsworth, UK: Penguin.

Bradbury, T. N., & Fincham, F. D. (1987). Affect and cognition in close relationships: Towards an integrative model. *Cognition and Emotion, 1,* 59-87.

Brennan, K. A., & Shaver, P. R. (1995). Dimensions of adult attachment, affect regulation, and romantic relationship functioning. *Personality and Social Psychology Bulletin, 21,* 267-283.

Brennan, K. A., Shaver, P. R., & Tobey, A. E. (1991). Attachment styles, gender and parental problem drinking. *Journal of Social and Personal Relationships, 8,* 451-466.

Bretherton, I. (1985). Attachment theory: Retrospect and prospect. *Monographs of the Society for Research in Child Development, 50*(1&2), 3-35.

Bretherton, I. (1987). New perspectives on attachment relations: Security, communication, and internal working models. In J. D. Osofsky (Ed.), *Handbook of infant development* (pp. 1061-1100). New York: John Wiley.

Bretherton, I. (1988). Open communication and internal working models: Their role in the development of attachment relationships. In *Nebraska Symposium on Motivation* (pp. 57-113). Lincoln: University of Nebraska Press.

Bretherton, I. (1992). The origins of attachment theory: John Bowlby and Mary Ainsworth. *Developmental Psychology, 28,* 759-775.

Buhrmester, D., & Furman, W. (1986). The changing functions of friends in childhood: A neo-Sullivanian perspective. In V. J. Derlega & B. A. Winstead (Eds.), *Friendships and social interaction* (pp. 41-62). New York: Springer.

Burns, D. D. (1980). *Feeling good: The new mood therapy.* New York: Signet.

Bus, A. G., & Van IJzendoorn, M. H. (1988). Mother-child interactions, attachment, and emergent literacy: A cross-sectional study. *Child Development, 59,* 1262-1272.

Cafferty, T. P., Davis, K. E., Medway, F. J., O'Hearn, R. E., & Chappell, K. D. (1994). Reunion dynamics among couples separated during Operation Desert Storm: An attachment theory analysis. In K. Bartholomew & D. Perlman (Eds.), *Advances in personal relationships* (Vol. 5, pp. 309-330). London: Jessica Kingsley.

Calkins, S. D., & Fox, N. A. (1992). The relations among infant temperament, security of attachment, and behavioral inhibition at twenty-four months. *Child Development, 63,* 1456-1472.

Campos, J. J., & Barrett, K. C. (1984). Toward a new understanding of emotions and their development. In C. E. Izard, J. Kagan, & R. B. Zajonc (Eds.), *Emotions, cognition and behavior* (pp. 229-263). Cambridge, UK: Cambridge University Press.

Cancian, F. M. (1987). *Love in America: Gender and self-development.* Cambridge, UK: Cambridge University Press.

Carlson, V., Cicchetti, D., Barnett, D., & Braunwald, K. (1989). Finding order in disorganization: Lessons from research on maltreated infants' attachments to their caregivers. In D. Cicchetti & V. Carlson (Eds.), *Child maltreatment: Theory and research on the causes and consequences of child abuse and neglect* (pp. 494-528). New York: Cambridge University Press.

Carnelley, K. B., & Janoff-Bulman, R. (1992). Optimism about love relationships: General vs. specific lessons from one's personal experiences. *Journal of Social and Personal Relationships, 9,* 5-20.

Carnelley, K. B., Pietromonaco, P. R., & Jaffe, K. (1994). Depression, working models of others, and relationship functioning. *Journal of Personality and Social Psychology, 66,* 127-140.

Carnelley, K. B., Pietromonaco, P. R., & Jaffe, K. (in press). Attachment, caregiving, and relationship functioning in couples: Effects of self and partner. *Personal Relationships.*

Carpenter, E. M., & Kirkpatrick, L. A. (1995). *Effects of attachment style and partner proximity on psychophysiological responses to stress.* Manuscript submitted for publication.

Christensen, A., & Sullaway, M. (1984). *Communication patterns questionnaire.* Unpublished manuscript, University of California, Los Angeles.

Clark, M. S., & Reis, H. T. (1988). Interpersonal processes in close relationships. *Annual Review of Psychology, 39,* 609-672.

Cohen, S. (1988). Psychosocial models of the role of social support in the etiology of physical disease. *Health Psychology, 7,* 269-297.

Collins, N. L. (in press). Working models of attachment: Implications for explanation, emotion and behavior. *Journal of Personality and Social Psychology.*

• Collins, N. L., & Read, S. J. (1990). Adult attachment, working models, and relationship quality in dating couples. *Journal of Personality and Social Psychology, 58,* 644-663.

Collins, N. L., & Read, S. J. (1994). Cognitive representations of attachment: The structure and function of working models. In K. Bartholomew & D. Perlman (Eds.), *Advances in personal relationships* (Vol. 5, pp. 53-90). London: Jessica Kingsley.

• Cox, M. J., Owen, M. T., Henderson, V. K., & Margand, N. A. (1992). Prediction of infant-father and infant-mother attachment. *Developmental Psychology, 28,* 474-483.

Crittenden, P. (1985). Social networks, quality of child-rearing, and child development. *Child Development, 56,* 1299-1313.

Crockenberg, S. B. (1981). Infant irritability, mother responsiveness, and social support influences on the security of infant-mother attachment. *Child Development, 52,* 857-865.

• Devine, P. G. (1989). Stereotypes and prejudice: Their automatic and controlled components. *Journal of Personality and Social Psychology, 56,* 5-18.

Douglas, J. D., & Atwell, F. C. (1988). *Love, intimacy, and sex.* Newbury Park, CA: Sage.

Egeland, B., & Farber, E. A. (1984). Infant-mother attachment: Factors related to its development and expression over time. *Child Development, 55,* 753-771.

Egeland, B., & Sroufe, L. (1981). Attachment and early maltreatment. *Child Development, 52,* 44-52.

Erickson, M. F., Sroufe, L. A., & Egeland, B. (1985). The relationship between quality of attachment and behavior problems in preschool in a high-risk sample. *Monographs of the Society for Research in Child Development, 50*(1&2), 147-166.

Escher-Graeub, D., & Grossmann, K. E. (1983). Bindungssicherheit im zweiten lebensjahr—die Regensburger Querschnittuntersuchung (Attachment security in the second year of life: the Regensburg cross-sectional study). University of Regensburg.

Feeney, B. C., & Kirkpatrick, L. A. (in press). The effects of adult attachment and presence of romantic partners on physiological responses to stress. *Journal of Personality and Social Psychology.*

Feeney, J. A. (1994). Attachment style, communication patterns and satisfaction across the life cycle of marriage. *Personal Relationships, 1,* 333-348.

Feeney, J. A. (1995a). Adult attachment and emotional control. *Personal Relationships, 2,* 143-159.

Feeney, J. A. (1995b). *Adult attachment and relationship-centered anxiety: Responses to physical and emotional distancing.* Unpublished manuscript, University of Queensland, Australia.

Feeney, J. A., & Noller, P. (1990). Attachment style as a predictor of adult romantic relationships. *Journal of Personality and Social Psychology, 58,* 281-291.

Feeney, J. A., & Noller, P. (1991). Attachment style and verbal descriptions of romantic partners. *Journal of Social and Personal Relationships, 8,* 187-215.

Feeney, J. A., & Noller, P. (1992). Attachment style and romantic love: Relationship dissolution. *Australian Journal of Psychology, 44*(2), 69-74.

Feeney, J. A., Noller, P., & Callan, V. J. (1994). Attachment style, communication and satisfaction in the early years of marriage. In K. Bartholomew & D. Perlman (Eds.), *Advances in personal relationships* (Vol. 5, pp. 269-308). London: Jessica Kingsley.

Feeney, J. A., Noller, P., & Hanrahan, M. (1994). Assessing adult attachment: Developments in the conceptualization of security and insecurity. In M. B. Sperling & W. H. Berman (Eds.), *Attachment in adults: Theory, assessment, and treatment* (pp. 128-152). New York: Guilford.

Feeney, J. A., Noller, P., & Patty, J. (1993). Adolescents' interactions with the opposite sex: Influence of attachment style and gender. *Journal of Adolescence, 16,* 169-186.

Feeney, J. A., & Ryan, S. M. (1994). Attachment style and affect regulation: Relationships with health behavior and family experiences of illness in a student sample. *Health Psychology, 13*, 334-345.

Fox, N. A., Kimmerly, N. L., & Schafer, W. D. (1991). Attachment to mother/attachment to father: A meta-analysis. *Child Development, 62*, 210-225.

Frijda, N. H. (1986). *The emotions.* Cambridge, UK: Cambridge University Press.

George, C., Kaplan, N., & Main, M. (1985). *The Attachment Interview for Adults.* Unpublished manuscript, University of California, Berkeley.

o Goldsmith, H. H., & Alansky, J. A. (1987). Maternal and infant temperamental predictors of attachment: A meta-analytic review. *Journal of Consulting and Clinical Psychology, 55*, 805-816.

Goossens, F. A., Van IJzendoorn, M. H., Tavecchio, L. W., & Kroonenberg, P. M. (1986). Stability of attachment across time and context in a Dutch sample. *Psychological Reports, 58*(1), 23-32.

Gottman, J. M., & Levenson, R. W. (1988). The social psychophysiology of marriage. In P. Noller & M. A. Fitzpatrick (Eds.), *Perspectives on marital interaction* (pp. 182-200). Clevedon: Multilingual Matters.

Greenberg, M. T., Siegel, J. M., & Leitch, C. J. (1983). The nature and importance of attachment relationships to parents and peers during adolescence. *Journal of Youth and Adolescence, 12*, 373-386.

Greenberg, M. T., & Speltz, M. L. (1988). Attachment and the ontogeny of conduct problems. In J. Belsky & T. Nezworski (Eds.), *Clinical implications of attachment* (pp. 177-218). Hillsdale, NJ: Lawrence Erlbaum.

Griffin , D. W., & Bartholomew, K. (1994). The metaphysics of measurement: The case of adult attachment. In K. Bartholomew & D. Perlman (Eds.), *Advances in personal relationships* (Vol. 5, pp. 17-52). London: Jessica Kingsley.

Grossmann, K. E., & Grossmann, K. (1984, September). *The development of conversational styles in the first year of life and its relationship to maternal sensitivity and attachment quality between mother and child.* Paper presented at the Congress of the German Society for Psychology, Vienna.

Grossmann, K. E., Grossmann, K., & Schwan, A. (1986). Capturing the wider view of attachment: A reanalysis of Ainsworth's Strange Situation. In C. E. Izard & P. B. Read (Eds.), *Measuring emotions in infants and children* (pp. 124-171). New York: Cambridge University Press.

₀ Grossmann, K., Grossmann, K. E., Spangler, G., Suess, G., & Unzner, L, (1985). Maternal sensitivity and newborns' orientation responses as related to quality of attachment in Northern Germany. *Monographs of the Society for Research in Child Development, 50*(1&2), 233-256.

Hammond, J. R., & Fletcher, G. J. O. (1991). Attachment styles and relationship satisfaction in the development of close relationships. *New Zealand Journal of Psychology, 20*(2), 56-62.

Hazan, C., & Shaver, P. R. (1987). Romantic love conceptualized as an attachment process. *Journal of Personality and Social Psychology, 52,* 511-524.

Hazan, C., & Shaver, P. R. (1990). Love and work: An attachment-theoretical perspective. *Journal of Personality and Social Psychology, 59,* 270-280.

Hazan, C., & Shaver, P. R. (1994). Attachment as an organizational framework for research on close relationships. *Psychological Inquiry,* 5(1), 1-22.

Hazan, C., & Zeifman, D. (1994). Sex and the psychological tether. In K. Bartholomew & D. Perlman (Eds.), *Advances in personal relationships* (Vol. 5, pp. 151-178). London: Jessica Kingsley.

Hazan, C., Zeifman, D., & Middleton, K. (1994, July). *Adult romantic attachment, affection, and sex.* Paper presented at the 7th International Conference on Personal Relationships, Groningen, The Netherlands.

Hazan, N. G., & Durrett, M. E. (1982). Relationship of security of attachment to exploration and cognitive mapping abilities in 2-year-olds. *Developmental Psychology, 18,* 751-759.

Hendrick, C., & Hendrick, S. S. (1986). A theory and method of love. *Journal of Personality and Social Psychology, 50,* 392-402.

Hendrick, C., Hendrick, S. S., Foote, F. H., & Slapion-Foote, M. J. (1984). Do men and women love differently? *Journal of Social and Personal Relationships, 1,* 177-195.

Hindy, C. G., & Schwartz, J. C. (1985, August). "Lovesickness" in dating relationships: An attachment perspective. Paper presented at the annual convention of the American Psychological Association, Los Angeles.

Isabella, R. A. (1993). Origins of attachment: Maternal interactive behavior across the first year. *Child Development, 64,* 605-621.

Isabella, R. A., & Belsky, J. (1991). Interactional synchrony and the origins of infant-mother attachment: A replication study. *Child Development, 62,* 373-384.

Isabella, R. A., Belsky, J., & von Eye, A. (1989). Origins of infant-mother attachment: An examination of interactional synchrony during the infant's first year. *Developmental Psychology, 25,* 12-21.

Izard, C. E., Haynes, O. M., Chisholm, G., & Baak, K. (1991). Emotional determinants of infant-mother attachment. *Child Development, 62,* 906-917.

Jacobvitz, D. B., & Burton, H. (1994, July). *Attachment process in mother-child relationships across generations.* Paper presented at the 7th International Conference on Personal Relationships, Groningen, The Netherlands.

Keelan, J. P. R, Dion, K. L., & Dion, K. K. (1994). Attachment style and heterosexual relationships among young adults: A short-term panel study. *Journal of Social and Personal Relationships, 11,* 201-214.

Kiecolt-Glaser, J. K., Malarkey, W. B., Chee, M., Newton, T., Cacioppo, J. T., Mao, H-Y., & Glaser, R. (1993). Negative behavior during marital conflict is associated with immunological down-regulation. *Psychosomatic Medicine, 55*, 395-409.

Kirkpatrick, L. A. (1992). An attachment-theory approach to the psychology of religion. *International Journal for the Psychology of Religion, 2*(1), 3-28.

Kirkpatrick, L. A. (1994). The role of attachment in religious belief and behavior. In K. Bartholomew & D. Perlman (Eds.), *Advances in personal relationships* (Vol. 5, pp. 239-265). London: Jessica Kingsley.

Kirkpatrick, L. A., & Davis, K. E. (1994). Attachment style, gender, and relationship stability: A longitudinal analysis. *Journal of Personality and Social Psychology, 66*, 502-512.

Kirkpatrick, L. A., & Hazan, C. (1994). Attachment styles and close relationships: A four-year prospective study. *Personal Relationships, 1*, 123-142.

Kirkpatrick, L. A., & Shaver, P. R. (1992). An attachment-theoretical approach to romantic love and religious belief. *Personality and Social Psychology Bulletin, 18*, 266-275.

Kobak, R. R., & Duemmler, S. (1994). Attachment and conversation: Toward a discourse analysis of adolescent and adult security. In K. Bartholomew & D. Perlman (Eds.), *Advances in personal relationships* (Vol. 5, pp. 121-149). London: Jessica Kingsley.

Kobak, R. R., & Hazan, C. (1991). Attachment in marriage: Effects of security and accuracy of working models. *Journal of Personality and Social Psychology, 60*, 861-869.

Kobak, R. R., & Sceery, A. (1988). Attachment in late adolescence: Working models, affect regulation, and representations of self and others. *Child Development, 59*, 135-146.

Kotler, T. (1985). Security and autonomy within marriage. *Human Relations, 38*, 299-321.

Kunce, L. J., & Shaver, P. R. (1994). An attachment-theoretical approach to caregiving in romantic relationships. In K. Bartholomew & D. Perlman (Eds.), *Advances in personal relationships* (Vol. 5, pp. 205-237). London: Jessica Kingsley.

Lamb, M. E. (1987). Predictive implications of individual differences in attachment. *Journal of Consulting and Clinical Psychology, 55*, 817-824.

Lamb, M. E., Thompson, R. A., Gardner, W. P., Charnov, E. L., & Estes, D. (1985). Security of infantile attachment as assessed in the strange situation: Its study and biological interpretation. *Annual Progress in Child Psychiatry and Development*, 53-114.

Lee, J. A. (1973). *The colors of love: An exploration of the ways of loving.* Ontario: New Press.

Lee, J. A. (1988). Love-styles. In R. J. Sternberg & M. Barnes (Eds.), *The psychology of love* (pp. 38-67). New Haven, CT: Yale University Press.

Levy, M. B., & Davis, K. E. (1988). Lovestyles and attachment styles compared: Their relations to each other and to various relationship characteristics. *Journal of Social and Personal Relationships, 5,* 439-471.

Lyons-Ruth, K., Alpern, L., & Repacholi, B. (1993). Disorganized infant attachment classification and maternal psychosocial problems as predictors of hostile-aggressive behavior in the preschool classroom. *Child Development, 64,* 572-585.

Main, M. (1983). Exploration, play, and cognitive functioning related to infant-mother attachment. *Infant Behavior and Development, 6,* 167-174.

Main, M., & Goldwyn, R. (1985). Adult attachment classification system. Unpublished manuscript, University of California, Berkeley.

Main, M., Kaplan, N., & Cassidy, J. (1985). Security in infancy, childhood, and adulthood: A move to the level of representation. *Monographs of the Society for Research in Child Development, 50*(1&2), 66-104.

Main, M., & Solomon, J. (1986). Discovery of an insecure disorganized/disoriented attachment pattern: Procedures, findings and implications for classification of behavior. In M. Yogman & T. B. Brazelton (Eds.), Affective development in infancy (pp. 95-124). Norwood, NJ: Ablex.

Main, M., Tomasini, L., & Tolan, W. (1979). Differences among mothers of infants judged to differ in security. *Developmental Psychology, 15,* 472-473.

Main, M., & Weston, D. R. (1981). The quality of the toddler's relationship to mother and to father: Related to conflict behavior and the readiness to establish new relationships. *Child Development, 52,* 932-940.

Mangelsdorf, S., Gunnar, M., Kestenbaum, R., Lang, S., & Andreas, D. (1990). Infant proneness-to-distress temperament, maternal personality, and mother-infant attachment: Associations and goodness of fit. *Child Development, 61,* 820-831.

Matas, L., Arend, R. A., & Sroufe, L. A. (1978). Continuity of adaptation in the second year: The relationship between quality of attachment and later competence. *Child Development, 49,* 547-556.

Mikulincer, M., Florian, V., & Tolmacz, R. (1990). Attachment styles and fear of personal death: A case study of affect regulation. *Journal of Personality and Social Psychology, 58,* 273-280.

Mikulincer, M., Florian, V., & Weller, A. (1993). Attachment styles, coping strategies, and posttraumatic psychological distress: The impact of the Gulf War in Israel. *Journal of Personality and Social Psychology, 64,* 817-826.

Mikulincer, M., & Nachshon, O. (1991). Attachment styles and patterns of self-disclosure. *Journal of Personality and Social Psychology, 61,* 321-331.

Miyake, K., Chen, S., & Campos, J. (1985). Infant temperament, mother's mode of interaction, and attachment in Japan: An interim report. *Monographs of the Society for Research in Child Development, 50*(1&2), 276-297.

Money, J. (1980). *Love and love sickness: The science of sex, gender difference, and pair-bonding.* Baltimore, MD: Johns Hopkins University Press.

Morris, D. (1982). Attachment and intimacy. In M. Fisher & G. Stricker (Eds.), *Intimacy* (pp. 305-323). New York: Plenum.

Noller, P. (1993). Gender and emotional communication in marriage: Different cultures or differential social power? *Journal of Language and Social Psychology, 12,* 92-112.

Noller, P., & Clarke, S. (1995, November). *Attachment to God: links of religion to attachment theory and mental health.* Paper presented at the National Council of Family Relations Conference, Portland, OR.

Noller, P., & Feeney, J. A. (1994). Whither attachment theory: Attachment to our caregivers or to our models? *Psychological Inquiry, 5*(1), 51-56.

Noller, P., & White, A. (1990). The validity of the Communication Patterns Questionnaire. *Psychological Assessment: A Journal of Consulting and Clinical Psychology, 2,* 478-482.

Parker, G. (1983). *Parental overprotection: A risk factor in psychosocial development.* New York: Grune & Stratton.

Parker, G. (1994). Parental bonding and depressive disorders. In M. B. Sperling & W. H. Berman (Eds.), *Attachment in adults: Theory, assessment, and treatment* (pp. 299-312). New York: Guilford.

Parker, G., Tupling, H., & Brown, L. B. (1979). A parental bonding instrument. *British Journal of Medical Psychology, 52*(1), 1-10.

Pederson, D. R., Moran, G., Sitko, C., Campbell, K., Ghesquire, K., & Acton, H. (1990). Maternal sensitivity and the security of infant-mother attachment: A Q-sort study. *Child Development, 61,* 1974-1983.

Peele, S. (1975). *Love and addiction.* New York: Taplinger.

Peele, S. (1988). Fools for love: The romantic ideal, psychological theory, and addictive love. In R. J. Sternberg & M. Barnes (Eds.), *The psychology of love* (pp. 159-188). New Haven, CT: Yale University Press.

• Pierce, G. R., Sarason, B. R., & Sarason, I. G. (1992). General and specific support expectations and stress as predictors of perceived supportiveness: An experimental study. *Journal of Personality and Social Psychology, 63,* 297-307.

Pietromonaco, P. R., & Carnelley, K. B. (1994). Gender and working models of attachment: Consequences for perceptions of self and romantic relationships. *Personal Relationships, 1,* 63-82.

Pistole, M. C. (1989). Attachment in adult romantic relationships: Style of conflict resolution and relationship satisfaction. *Journal of Social and Personal Relationships, 6,* 505-510.

Radke-Yarrow, M., Cummings, E. M., Kuczynski, L., & Chapman, M. (1985). Patterns of attachment in two- and three-year-olds in normal families and families with parental depression. *Child Development, 56,* 884-893.

Rahim, M. A. (1983). A measure of styles of handling interpersonal conflict. *Academy of Management Journal, 26,* 368-376.

Rice, K. G. (1990). Attachment in adolescence: A narrative and meta-analytic review. *Journal of Youth and Adolescence, 19,* 511-538.

Richman, J., & Flaherty, J. A. (1987). Adult psychosocial assets and depressive mood over time: Effects of internalized childhood attachments. *Journal of Nervous and Mental Disease, 175,* 703-712.

Ricks, M. H. (1985). The social transmission of parental behavior: Attachment across generations. *Monographs of the Society for Research in Child Development, 50*(1&2), 211-227.

Ricks, M. H., & Noyes, D. (1984). *Secure babies have secure mothers.* Unpublished manuscript, University of Massachusetts-Amherst.

Roggman, L. A., Langlois, J. H., & Hubbs-Tait, L. (1987). Mothers, infants, and toys: Social play correlates of attachment. *Infant Behavior and Development, 10,* 233-237.

Rothbard, J. C., & Shaver, P. R. (1994). Continuity of attachment across the life span. In M. B. Sperling & W. H. Berman (Eds.), *Attachment in adults: Theory, assessment, and treatment* (pp. 31-71). New York: Guilford.

Rubenstein, C., & Shaver, P. (1982). *In search of intimacy.* New York: Delacorte.

Rubin, Z. (1973). *Liking and loving: An invitation to social psychology.* New York: Holt, Rinehart, & Winston.

Sagi, A., Van IJzendoorn, M. H., & Koren-Karie, N. (1991). Primary appraisal of the strange situation: A cross-cultural analysis of preseparation episodes. *Developmental Psychology, 27,* 587-596.

Schaap, C., Buunk, B., & Kerkstra, A. (1988). Marital conflict resolution. In P. Noller & M. A. Fitzpatrick (Eds.), *Perspective on marital interaction* (p. 219). Clevedon, England: Miltilingual Matters. (Reprinted by permission)

Scharfe, E., & Bartholomew, K. (1994). Reliability and stability of adult attachment patterns. *Personal Relationships, 1,* 23-43.

Senchak, M., & Leonard, K. E. (1992). Attachment styles and marital adjustment among newlywed couples. *Journal of Social and Personal Relationships, 9,* 51-64.

Shaver, P. R., & Brennan, K. A. (1992). Attachment styles and the "big five" personality traits: Their connections with each other and with romantic relationship outcomes. *Personality and Social Psychology Bulletin, 18,* 536-545.

Shaver, P. R., & Hazan, C. (1988). A biased overview of the study of love. *Journal of Social and Personal Relationships, 5,* 473-501.

Shaver, P. R., & Hazan, C. (1993). Adult romantic attachment: Theory and evidence. In D. Perlman & W. Jones (Eds.), *Advances in personal relationships* (Vol. 4, pp. 29-70). London: Jessica Kingsley.

Shaver, P. R., Hazan, C., & Bradshaw, D. (1988). Love as attachment: The integration of three behavioral systems. In R. J. Sternberg & M. Barnes (Eds.), *The psychology of love* (pp. 68-99). New Haven, CT: Yale University Press.

Simpson, J. A. (1990). Influence of attachment styles on romantic relationships. *Journal of Personality and Social Psychology, 59,* 971-980.

Simpson, J. A., & Rholes, W. S. (1994). Stress and secure base relationships in adulthood. In K. Bartholomew & D. Perlman (Eds.), *Advances in personal relationships* (Vol. 5, pp. 181-204). London: Jessica Kingsley.

• Simpson, J. A., Rholes, W. S., & Nelligan, J. S. (1992). Support seeking and support giving within couples in an anxiety-provoking situation: The role of attachment styles. *Journal of Personality and Social Psychology, 62,* 434-446.

Sperling, M. B. (1985). Discriminant measures for desperate love. *Journal of Personality Assessment, 49,* 324-328.

Sperling, M. B., & Lyons, L. S. (1994). Representations of attachment and psychotherapeutic change. In M. B. Sperling & W. H. Berman (Eds.), *Attachment in adults: Theory, assessment, and treatment* (pp. 331-347). New York: Guilford.

Spieker, S. J. (1986). Patterns of very insecure attachment found in samples of high-risk infants and toddlers. *Topics in Early Childhood Special Education, 6,* 37-53.

Sprecher, S., & McKinney, K. (1993). *Sexuality.* Newbury Park, CA: Sage.

Sroufe, L. A. (1979). The coherence of individual development: Early care, attachment, and subsequent developmental issues. *American Psychologist, 34,* 834-841.

Sroufe, L. A. (1988). The role of infant-caregiver attachment in development. In J. Belsky & T. Nezworski (Eds.), *Clinical implications of attachment* (pp. 18-38). Hillsdale, NJ: Lawrence Erlbaum.

Sroufe, L. A., & Fleeson, J. (1986). Attachment and the construction of relationships. In W. W. Hartup & Z. Rubin (Eds.), *Relationships and development* (pp. 51-71). Hillsdale, NJ: Lawrence Erlbaum.

Sroufe, L. A., Schork, E., Motti, F., Lawroski, N., & LaFreniere, P. (1984). The role of affect in social competence. In C. E. Izard, J. Kagan, & R. B. Zajonc (Eds.), *Emotions, cognition, and behavior* (pp. 289-319). New York: Cambridge University Press.

֍ Sroufe, L. A., & Waters, E. (1977). Attachment as an organizational construct. *Child Development, 48,* 1184-1199.

Sternberg, R. J. (1986). A triangular theory of love. *Psychological Review, 93,* 119-135.

Strahan, B. J. (1991). Attachment theory and family functioning: Expectations and congruencies. *Australian Journal of Marriage and Family, 12*(1), 12-26.

Strahan, B. J. (1995). Predictors of depression: An attachment theoretical approach. *Journal of Family Studies, 1*(1), 33-47.

Tennov, D. (1979). *Love and limerence: The experience of being in love.* New York: Stein & Day.

Thompson, R. A., Connell, J. P., & Bridges, L. J. (1988). Temperament, emotion, and social interactive behavior in the strange situation: A component process analysis of attachment system functioning. *Child Development, 59,* 1102-1110.

Thompson, R. A., & Lamb, M. E. (1983). Security of attachment and stranger sociability in infancy. *Developmental Psychology, 19,* 184-191.

Van den Boom, D. (1990). Preventive intervention and the quality of mother-infant interaction and infant exploration in irritable infants. In W. Koops, H. J. G. Soppe, J. L. Van der Linden, P. C. M. Molenaar, & J. J. F. Schroots (Eds.), *Developmental psychology behind the dikes: An outline of developmental psychology research in the Netherlands.* The Netherlands: Uitgeverij Eburon.

Van IJzendoorn, M. H., & Kroonenberg, P. M. (1988). Cross-cultural patterns of attachment: A meta-analysis of the strange situation. *Child Development, 59,* 147-156.

Vaughn, B., Egeland, B., Sroufe, L. A., & Waters, E. (1979). Individual differences in infant-mother attachment at twelve and eighteen months: Stability and change in families under stress. *Child Development, 50,* 971-975.

Vaughn, B. E., Lefever, G. B., Seifer, R., & Barglow, P. (1989). Attachment behavior, attachment security, and temperament during infancy. *Child Development, 60,* 728-737.

Vaughn, B. E., Stevenson-Hinde, J., Waters, E., Kotsaftis, A., Lefever, G. B., Shouldice, A., Trudel, M., & Belsky, J. (1992). Attachment security and temperament in infancy and early childhood: Some conceptual clarifications. *Developmental Psychology, 28,* 463-473.

Vaux, A. (1988). *Social support: Theory, research, and intervention.* New York: Praeger.

Vormbrock, J. K. (1993). Attachment theory as applied to wartime and job-related marital separation. *Psychological Bulletin, 114*(1), 122-144.

Waters, E. (1978). The reliability and stability of individual differences in infant-mother attachment. *Child Development, 49,* 483-494.

Waters, E., Wippman, J., & Sroufe, L. A. (1979). Attachment, positive affect, and competence in the peer group: Two studies in construct validation. *Child Development, 50,* 821-829.

Watson, D., & Pennebaker, J. W. (1989). Health complaints, stress, and distress: Exploring the central role of negative affectivity. *Psychological Review, 96,* 234-254.

Watzlawick, P. (1983). *The situation is hopeless, but not serious: The pursuit of unhappiness.* New York: Norton.

Weiss, R. S. (1982). Attachment in adult life. In C. M. Parkes & J. Stevenson-Hinde (Eds.), *The place of attachment in human behavior* (pp. 171-184). New York: Basic Books.

Weiss, R. S. (1986). Continuities and transformations in social relationships from childhood to adulthood. In W. W. Hartup & Z. Rubin (Eds.), *Relationships and development* (pp. 95-110). Hillsdale, NJ: Lawrence Erlbaum.

Weiss, R. S. (1991). The attachment bond in childhood and adulthood. In C. M. Parkes, J. Stevenson-Hinde, & P. Marris (Eds.), *Attachment across the life cycle* (pp. 66-76). London: Tavistock/Routledge.

West, M., Livesley, W. J., Reiffer, L., & Sheldon, A. (1986). The place of attachment in the life events model of stress and illness. *Canadian Journal of Psychiatry, 31,* 202-207.

Youngblade, L. M., & Belsky, J. (1992). Parent-child antecedents of 5-year-olds' close friendships: A longitudinal analysis. *Developmental Psychology, 28,* 700-713.

Author Index

163

Subject Index

About the Authors

Judith Feeney is Lecturer in Psychology at the University of Queensland in Brisbane. She obtained a PhD at the same university in 1991, having previously worked in teaching and counseling positions with a variety of client groups. Her research interests include marital and family relationships (especially attachment relationships), interpersonal communication, and the link between personal relationships and health. She has published a number of widely cited articles and book chapters in these areas.

Patricia Noller received a PhD from the University of Queensland in 1981 and is Professor of Psychology at the university. She has published extensively in the area of marital and family relationships, including attachment relationships. She received an Early Career Award from the Australian Psychological Society and is a

175

Fellow of the Academy of the Social Sciences in Australia. She is foundation editor of *Personal Relationships: Journal of the International Society for the Study of Personal Relationships.*